OKANAGAN COLLEGE LIBRARY

7

Africa in the N

ABOUT TI

The books in this series are an initiative by CODESRIA, the Council for the Development of Social Science Research in Africa, to encourage African scholarship relevant to the multiple intellectual, policy and practical problems and opportunities confronting the African continent in the twenty-first century.

CODESRIA in association with Zed Books

Titles in the series:

African Intellectuals: Rethinking Politics, Language, Gender and Development edited by Thandika Mkandawire (2005)

Urban Africa: Changing Contours of Survival in the City edited by A. M. Simone and A. Abouhani (2005)

Liberal Democracy and Its Critics in Africa: Political Dysfunction and the Struggle for Social Progress edited by Tukumbi Lumumba-Kasongo (2005)

Negotiating Modernity: Africa's Ambivalent Experience edited by Elísio Salvado Macamo (2005)

Africa and Development Challenges in the New Millennium: The NEPAD Debate edited by J. O. Adésínà, A. Olukoshi and Yao Graham (2006)

Insiders and Outsiders: Citizenship and Xenophobia in Contemporary Southern Africa Francis B. Nyamnjoh (2006)

African Anthropologies: History, Critique and Practice edited by Mwenda Ntarangwi, David Mills and Mustafa Babiker (2006)

Intellectuals and African Development: Pretension and Resistance in African Politics edited by Björn Beckman and Gbemisola Adeoti (2006)

Kenya: The Struggle for Democracy edited by Godwin R. Murunga and Shadrack W. Nasong'o (2007)

Ghana: One Decade of the Liberal State edited by Kwame Boafo-Arthur (2007)

African Literature as Political Philosophy MSC Okolo (2007)

About CODESRIA

The Council for the Development of Social Science Research in Africa (CODESRIA) is an independent organization whose principal objectives are facilitating research, promoting research-based publishing and creating multiple forums geared towards the exchange of views and information among African researchers. It challenges the fragmentation of research through the creation of thematic research networks that cut across linguistic and regional boundaries.

CODESRIA publishes a quarterly journal, *Africa Development*, the longest-standing Africa-based social science journal; *Afrika Zamani*, a journal of history; the *African Sociological Review*, *African Journal of International Affairs* (AJIA), *Africa Review of Books* and the *Journal of Higher Education in Africa*. It co-publishes *Identity, Culture and Politics: An Afro-Asian Dialogue*, and *Africa Media Review*. Research results and other activities of the institution are disseminated through 'Working Papers', 'Monograph Series', 'CODESRIA Book Series', and the *CODESRIA Bulletin*.

About the author

MSC Okolo was educated at the University of Calabar, and then at the University of Ibadan where she received her PhD in Philosophy. She also has a PGD in Public Relations. A Civitella Ranieri Fellow, she is the author of *Winds on my Mind* and *Leaps of Faith* and has contributed to many short story and poetry anthologies. Her short story 'Those Days' won a Liberty Merchant Bank Prize. Her PhD thesis won the CODESRIA Doctoral Prize in 2005.

OKANAGAN COLLEGE
LIBRARY
BRITISH COLUMBIA

MSC Okolo

African literature as political philosophy

CODESRIA Books
DAKAR

in association with

Zed Books
LONDON · NEW YORK

African literature as political philosophy was first published in 2007
by Zed Books Ltd, 7 Cynthia Street, London N1 9JF, UK and Room 400,
175 Fifth Avenue, New York, NY 10010, USA
<www.zedbooks.co.uk>

in association with CODESRIA, Avenue Cheikh Anta Diop, X Canal IV,
BP 3304, Dakar, 18524, Senegal
<www.codesria.org>

Copyright © CODESRIA, 2007

CODESRIA would like to express its gratitude to the Swedish
International Development Agency (SIDA/SAREC), the International
Development Research Centre (IDRC), Ford Foundation, MacArthur
Foundation, Carnegie Corporation, the Norwegian Ministry of Foreign
Affairs, the Danish Agency for International Development (DANIDA),
the French Ministry of Co-operation, the United Nations Development
Programme (UNDP), the Netherlands Ministry of Foreign Affairs,
Rockefeller Foundation, FINIDA, NORAD, CIDA, IIEP/ADEA, OECD,
IFS, OXFAM America, UN/UNICEF and the Government of Senegal for
supporting its research, training and publication programmes.

The right of MSC Okolo to be identified as the author of this work
has been asserted by her in accordance with the Copyright, Designs
and Patents Act, 1988.

Cover designed by Andrew Corbett
Set in Sabon and Gill Sans Heavy by Ewan Smith, London
Index: <ed.emery@britishlibrary.net>
Printed and bound in Malta by Gutenberg Press Ltd

Distributed in the USA exclusively by Palgrave Macmillan, a division
of St Martin's Press, LLC, 175 Fifth Avenue, New York, NY 10010.

A catalogue record for this book is available from the British Library.
US CIP data are available from the Library of Congress.

All rights reserved

No part of this publication may be reproduced, stored in a retrieval
system or transmitted, in any form or by any means, electronic or
otherwise, without the prior permission of the publisher.

ISBN 978 1 84277 894 4 hb (Zed Books)
ISBN 978 1 84277 895 1 pb (Zed Books)

ISBN 978 2 86978 204 4 pb (CODESRIA)

Contents

Acknowledgements

The publication of this book began with the CODESRIA Doctoral Prize (2005) awarded to my thesis: *Exploring Literature as Political Philosophy through a Comparative Study of Chinua Achebe and Ngugi wa Thiong'o*. The present volume retains all the essentials of this thesis, albeit with minor modifications in content and form. I am immensely grateful to CODESRIA for supporting the publication of this work.

The writing of a PhD thesis is dependent on the encouragement and support of many people. While I cannot list all of them, I am deeply grateful to my supervisors Felix A. Adeigbo and, especially, Segun Oladipo, whose comments, criticism and direction were crucially important. I would also like to thank Ngugi wa Thiong'o for granting me an interview via the Internet. My colleagues, the late Chris Uroh, Joe Ushie, Tunde Awosunmi, Dom Danjibo, Lwazi Lushaba and Kunle Okesipe, offered helpful comments. I am also grateful to my teachers at the University of Calabar for starting me on a firm foundation.

The kindness of Terry Olowu, Carol Etim and Mrs Usendie made a critical difference to my wellbeing. Oiza Dominic, Perp Agbi, Alex Shenge, Chiaka Anumudu, Ifeanyi Itodo, Uche Nnodu and the Rev. Fathers Chris Oranyeli and Emeka Nwosu were also of great assistance to me.

I am grateful to my brothers and sisters, who have always supported me. I also thank my in-laws, especially my mother-in-law, Christie Nwakaeme, for their encouragement.

My husband Nnadozie Nwakaeme and our little son Chidalu Chukwuekee, through daily acts of kindness and love, made it easy to bring this book to a conclusion, without the strains that ordinarily accompany such projects. My husband's death on 14 November 2006 and our daughter Kaosisochi's birth on 29 September 2006 is a difficult balance of sorrow and joy.

I dedicate this book to the memory of my parents, Cecilia Ogbonne Okolo (who died on 15 March 2004 while waiting for me to defend my PhD thesis ... this is it, Mama) and Felix Aka Okolo, who died on 7 January 1980 believing that I would one day become a medical doctor (I hope this somewhat suffices, Papa).

Abbreviations

AGOW	*A Grain of Wheat*
AMOP	*A Man of the People*
AOG	*Arrow of God*
ASUU	Academic Staff Union of Universities
DOC	*Devil on the Cross*
NASU	Non-Academic Staff Union
NEPAD	New Partnership for Africa's Development
NLAE	*No Longer at Ease*
TFA	*Things Fall Apart*
TRB	*The River Between*
WNC	*Weep Not, Child*

In memory of Mama and Papa,
who taught me perseverance,
merit and love for life

ONE
Introduction: a neglected benefit

§ The recognition that there is an affinity between literature and philosophy and, by implication, political philosophy, is not new. As theoretical disciplines concerned with raising social consciousness, philosophy and literature engage in similar speculation about the good society and what is good for humanity. They influence thoughts about political currents and conditions. They can, for instance, lead the reader to critical reflections on the type of leaders suitable for a given society and on the degree of civic consciousness exercised by the people in protecting their rights. Philosophy and literature, equally, offer critical evaluation of existing and possible forms of political arrangements, beliefs and practices. In addition, they provide insights into political concepts and justification for normative judgements about politics and society. They also create awareness of possibilities for change.

Yet the benefits of the interface between African philosophy and literature are not frequently explored. The search for orientations in African philosophy neglected the importance of literary works in the construction of African ideology. This neglect is evident in the kind of recognition accorded to philosophy and literature as a course in philosophy departments in African universities. When it is taught at all, it is often offered merely as an option.

The quest for a dialogue between philosophy and literature is timely, given the political crisis confronting African societies and the consequent need to re-establish the basis of order in these societies. The imaginative writer, through his or her work, can offer critical appraisal of the existing political situation and in this way can mould or redirect the actions of society, its beliefs and values. As such, ideas contained in literature can influence people's perception about politics and about the best means of effecting political change.

By prompting people to seek justification for and to criticize their political situation, literature also performs a normative function. The imaginative writer through his or her work can set an ideal standard for society and the state. An imaginative writer can thus perform the function of political philosophy: to disseminate ideas significant for the understanding of politics in a given socio-cultural context. Achebe expresses this idea thus: 'An African creative writer who tries to avoid the big social and political issues of contemporary Africa will end up being completely irrelevant' (Achebe 1975: 78).

It is the aim of this book to show how a philosophical reading of literature can be of immense benefit in promoting African self-understanding by providing an intellectual and analytical framework within which the African experience can be conceptualized, interpreted and reorganized. To effect this, literary works dealing with political issues, specifically, Chinua Achebe's *Anthills of the Savannah* (Achebe 1987), hereafter referred to as *Anthills*, and Ngugi wa Thiong'o's *Petals of Blood* (Ngugi wa Thiong'o 1977), hereafter referred to as *Petals*, have been chosen for study.

The choice of Achebe and Ngugi is based on recognition of the fact that they have explored the African experience within the context of ideas that can be discussed and analysed. Equally, *Anthills* and *Petals* have been singled out for particular attention because of their insightful portrayal of the political situation in Africa. They also offer views on political reconstruction, a search for a new order in Africa.

Achebe, in *Anthills*, identifies the dominant problems preventing Africa from achieving social transformation, ascribing them to internal factors initiated and perpetuated by Africans themselves. In his work the activities of civil servants, urban employees of public corporations and students contribute more to perpetuating underdevelopment in African societies than do external factors. The solution is to adopt a political ideology that welcomes different ideas, a reformist agenda that aims at a gradual but consistent approach. Leaders must also act as role models. Ngugi, on the other hand, identifies imperialist capitalism as Africa's bane. As a solution, he suggests transformation of African societies in line with Marxist ideology, which accepts revolutionary violence as entirely justified, and proposes socialism and a classless society as means of resolving Africa's problems.

The differences in these writers' respective positions serve to highlight the inadequacies of each and to underscore the complex nature of the African political predicament. Appeal is made to a higher synthesis that transcends and harmonizes the essentials of their divergent views and goes beyond them to incorporate what both may have missed, providing a new course of social reconstruction for Africa.

It is hoped that the present work will contribute in the following areas: helping to highlight the immense benefit that might accrue from a philosophical engagement with literature; pointing up how the exploration of African philosophy through African literature might help to enrich African philosophy; assisting in showing how the investigation of literature can promote African self-understanding; and helping to provide insight into the relationship between literature and society in Africa. It is hoped, too, that it will add to the knowledge of how literature, specifically *Anthills* and *Petals*, throws significant light on the possibilities for social change in Africa, and also that it will add to the increasing demand for a practical mission for African philosophy in the contemporary world. Finally, it is hoped that it might serve to promote intellectual cross-fertilization between disciplines.

Outline of the book

The book is divided into seven chapters, the first this Introduction. Chapter 2 serves to establish a theoretical basis for the study. The following issues are discussed: first, a characterization of the senses in which philosophy and literature are employed; second, the affinity between philosophy and literature; and finally, a discussion on literature as political philosophy.

Chapter 3 focuses on Chinua Achebe and Ngugi wa Thiong'o as political thinkers, providing a theoretical basis for judging their works as political philosophy, and giving the rationale for a subsequent critical examination of *Anthills* and *Petals* as works of political philosophy. Two tasks are undertaken here: first, a discussion on the political thinkers in general, and second, a discussion on Achebe and Ngugi as political thinkers.

Achebe's reformist agenda in *Anthills* is the subject of Chapter 4. Achebe's portrayal of Africa's political situation and his ideas concerning the sort of ideology considered most appropriate for reordering African society are evaluated.

Ngugi's Marxist aesthetic is explored in Chapter 5, which aims to show how *Petals* functions as a fictional account of Marx's ideology of class struggle; the organization of workers through unions; the transformation of society through an inevitable revolution that will sweep away capitalism and all the oppressive tools it has used to enslave, divide, disunite, suppress and exploit the proletariat; and the eventual triumph of communism, presented as the ideal ideology to pursue in the transformation of African societies. Of course, with the fall of communism in Eastern Europe, Marxism faces a great challenge: to demonstrate its continued relevance as a political creed. Ngugi's ideology is also evaluated in this light.

Chapter 6 offers comparative analyses of Achebe's and Ngugi's perspectives on the African condition. Their opposing views on some

3

key issues – class analysis, dependency and leadership – are also critically assessed.

The conclusion, Chapter 7, is a reflection on how the essentials of Achebe's and Ngugi's divergent views can be harmonized and what they failed to include incorporated in an attempt to find a new course for social reconstruction in Africa. My point is that an aggregate acceptance of either Achebe's or Ngugi's ideology will obscure important differences across the continent. What is needed is an open-minded, analytical approach that allows for serious interrogation of the process, the institutions and agency that make up Africa's political life in such a manner that individual African states are allowed the freedom to make necessary subtractions, additions, remodifications and, even, divisions.

TWO

Literature as philosophy: a theoretical framework

§ In building a theoretical framework for this book, it is necessary to start with conceptual clarifications, to prevent any misunderstanding, especially in the case of philosophy, where there is little consensus as to what it means. To achieve this, this chapter will attempt to establish the senses in which philosophy and literature are employed, it will define the affinity between philosophy and literature, and lastly, it will undertake a discussion on literature as political philosophy before examining pertinent examples.

Philosophy

It is a general belief that the word 'philosophy' has no universally accepted definition; philosophers are not in agreement about what the enterprise of philosophy should *be* – its nature, scope, method, limitations and so on. Nevertheless, there is a useful way of attempting to understand what philosophy is: an examination of some of its key concerns. These are the love of wisdom; the formulation of a worldview; a clarification or analysis of concepts and/or arguments; and a critical evaluation of ideas.

The love of wisdom This conception of philosophy is based on its etymology, the word 'philosophy' being derived from the Greek word *philosophia*, which means 'love of' (*philo-*), and 'wisdom or knowledge' (*sophia*). Western philosophy is said to have started with the Greeks because they are reputed to have been the first civilization to demonstrate this love of knowledge by posing the fundamental questions about the basic 'stuff' of all things.

Equally, Socrates is regarded by many as the model of a philosopher because of his relentless pursuit of knowledge. He openly confessed that he was ignorant but willing to learn. Even when the Delphi oracle declared him the wisest man in Greece, he still interpreted this to mean that he was wiser than other wise men because he was aware of his ignorance. Philosophy understood from this standpoint is the pursuit of knowledge – an attempt to probe underneath the surface of things.

The formulation of a worldview Among the common issues that engage philosophers are the following questions. What are the meaning and purpose of life? Is reality something physical or something grasped by mind alone? What is the relationship between the mind and the body? What is the true nature of justice? Can mankind be both free and subject to authority? These questions can be summed up as an examination of the basic questions concerning mankind and the purpose(s) of existence. What distinguishes a philosophical worldview is its generality and the use of reason, the rigour, the conscious or reflective effort that philosophers put into its formulation in an attempt to get at the real nature of things in so far as mankind can apprehend them.

Some of the distinguishing features of a philosophical worldview are worth highlighting. The first is that issues discussed in philosophy are of a general nature. This means that when philosophers are engaged in an issue, for instance, the mind–body problem, their interest is not limited to, say, Mr A's mind and body but to the relationship that exists between the mind and body of mankind in general. Socrates' concern with virtue, likewise, is not addressed to a particular man but to mankind in general.

The second point to highlight is that philosophers rely on reason in order to advance their points of view; philosophy is a rational inquiry and so philosophers do not admit superstitious beliefs, dogmas, supernatural revelation or any form of 'given truth' into their enterprise.

The third point is that the philosophic enterprise is a rigorous and conscious or reflective one. Philosophers strive to account for the real nature of any given thing as far as mankind can apprehend it. Philosophers are not easily satisfied with an answer, nor do they accept a view they know is inadequate. So long as it is reasonable to offer alternative explanations to a given phenomenon, philosophers will continue probing. Some examples will help to illustrate this point.

Plato's idealism follows from a systematic reasoning that the world can be bifurcated – the world of Forms and the world of Appearance (Plato 1941: 179–89). The world of Appearance imitates the world of Forms and the essence of philosophy is to reconnect the mind to reality. Aristotle disagreed with this on the basis that the Forms do not exist independently of physical things. If physical things imitate the Forms, then it follows logically that the Forms exist in things (Aristotle 1965a). Reality becomes not a transcendental Form but the physical objects manifesting Form.

Descartes employed a more stringent approach in carrying out his

6

philosophical inquiry. For him, reality is neither Form nor the physical objects manifesting Form, but rather something that a rational agent will regard as indubitable (Descartes 1997). Thus, by a conscious denial of all knowledge he had acquired, he was able to arrive at a basic truth that he could not deny: the fact that he thinks.

Locke rejected the notion that the human mind can arrive at a basic truth by critically assessing the intellectual powers of man (Locke 1947). He reasoned that knowledge is based on the objects we experience. As such, the origin of ideas is not Plato's esoteric Form or Cartesian mind divested of all experience, but experience itself, which manifests in two ways, sensation and reflection. It is through the senses that we first get our ideas before the mind can reflect on them.

For Marx, all the above efforts to interpret the world, although important to philosophy, are not the whole of it. Accordingly, he declared that although philosophers may have interpreted the world in many ways, the point is to *change* it.[1] Marx arrived at his view following a keen observation of historical processes. He reasoned that the economic wellbeing of mankind is all-important because this is what guides consciousness.

A clarification or analysis of concepts and/or arguments A main concern of philosophy is with ideas. In order to assess these ideas to find out if they should be accepted, modified or rejected, it is necessary to understand clearly the terms used in conveying them.

For instance, our present attempt to show how philosophy is to be understood in this book underscores the necessity for clarification. Without embarking on this exercise, a reader can interpret 'philosophy' in whatever sense he or she chooses, including interpreting it in the 'ordinary' sense, to mean a view that underlies what a person is doing, as when a cook talks about the 'philosophy of good cooking'.

Small wonder that some philosophers (Bertrand Russell, G. E. Moore and Ludwig Wittgenstein) see clarification or analysis of concepts as the main business of philosophy; most problems in philosophy are seen as arising from employing words inaccurately. In addition, to identify the meaning of a concept requires analysis of terms. In this way, language plays a vital role in the conception of philosophy. Ordinary language is seen as responsible for philosophical problems because it obscures meaning, and to resolve this problem, philosophy undertakes analysis of language. Its challenge becomes how to translate ordinary language into logically adequate language.

7

The logical positivists attempted to meet this challenge, dismissing metaphysics as meaningless on the basis that its language did not consist of sentences that corresponded with actual observations. Wittgenstein, who had advocated, in his *Tractatus logico-philosophicus*, the abandoning of metaphysics because it is meaningless, influenced them. Unlike Wittgenstein, however, the logical positivists declared what the content of a logically adequate language should consist of. For them, language should record actual observations; the factual meaning of a proposition depends only on its verifiability by the senses. This gave birth to their verification principle.

The view that philosophy is all about clarification or analysis of concepts, however, needs to be evaluated. How is the concept 'clarification of concepts' itself to be clarified? Parkinson (1988: 8) observes that 'clarity seems to be a relative matter, in that what may be clear to one person may not be clear to another'. In this way, clarity cannot be something absolute in the sense propagated by its champions. The logical positivists' position that verification is the all-important condition for a meaningful proposition also fails to clarify how verification itself can be verified. For instance, can the verification principle be either analytically or empirically verified? If it passes the test of analytic verification, then it would be uninformative and tautological. In this sense, it would lose its relevance as a test of meaning because it would never enrich our knowledge of the world. If, on the other hand, it is empirically verifiable, then it would itself require verification.

Besides, the assertion of the logical positivists that the meaning of a proposition depends only on its verifiability by the senses is not a scientific proposition: there is no way to test it through observation. As such the charge of the logical positivists that metaphysics is meaningless because its assertions cannot be empirically verified can also apply to their own position.

It is, therefore, not surprising that the logical positivists tried to save their position by using Carnap's Principle of Tolerance. This principle recognizes the need not to set up stringent standards but to put forward suggestions or recommendations that might be accepted. Equally, Wittgenstein, in his *Philosophical Investigations*, published posthumously in 1953, reviewed his position that a 'name' must correspond to the object it stood for in meaning. Instead he opined that philosophical problems arise when people have a false picture of the way language works. Attention should be paid to the meaning terms have in particular contexts rather than imposing some kind of antecedent standard of meaningfulness on language. The business of the philosopher, therefore, is to expose this false view about language.

A. J. Ayer also found it necessary to change his position that philosophy should be about clarification and analysis, extending the business of philosophy to asking questions about justification (Ayer 1976: 45–57). Parkinson (1988: 13) notes that this shift of interest from questions about meaning to questions about justification has greatly influenced recent political philosophy. Political issues, such as the demand for human rights, are viewed from the point of justifiability.

The shortcomings of clarification notwithstanding, it is important to note that through conceptual clarifications many pseudo-problems are eliminated. Even in political philosophy there is need not just to seek justification but to be clear on the use of concepts. Bodunrin's assertion (1981b: 22) that 'if one of the things we want to do is to achieve consistency in our set of beliefs, then eliminative arguments are indispensable', perhaps best sums up this position.

The critical evaluation of ideas Philosophy embodies the quest to reflect critically on our ideas and experiences. The attempt of the early Greek philosophers to account for the ultimate substance of all things is one such instance of critical reflection. Their observation of the diversity and the unity in the universe led them to the search for answers to some fundamental questions. It is important to note that the answers they arrived at were different as each tried critically to evaluate the others' positions. For instance, Anaximander rejected Thales' choice of water as the basic element on the grounds that water was no more basic than earth, air or fire. He reasoned that if all four were basic, then they should limit each other and, as such, none could be ultimate. This led him to the conclusion that the ultimate stuff could not be physical but the boundless, within which is contained all that is physical.

Philosophical reflection can also begin with the human person. Some of the issues that daily confront mankind are the purpose of existence, the span of life, relationship to other creatures, happiness and pain, sadness and joy. Socrates called attention to the need for mankind critically to question and reflect on issues in life, insisting that the unexamined life is not worth living.

From this viewpoint, philosophy as a critical reflection questions mankind's conception of life with a view to providing new ways of understanding existence. Criticism here is applied in the sense Staniland used it to mean:

9

not negative appraisal, but rational, impartial and articulate appraisal whether positive or negative. To be 'critical' of received ideas is accordingly not the same thing as rejecting them: it consists rather in seriously asking oneself whether the ideas in question should be reformed, modified or conserved, and in applying one's entire intellectual and imaginative intelligence to the search for an answer. (Staniland 1979: 4)

Philosophy thus becomes 'the attempt to give rational grounds for accepting or rejecting certain beliefs which we normally take for granted' (Raphael 1976: 4).

Socrates' aim, for instance, in asking questions was not merely to expose people's ignorance but to provoke critical assessment of existing conditions that might help mankind in the search for knowledge. The insistence of some African philosophers that African philosophy can emerge out of the critical works of professional philosophers shows the need for a critical approach to philosophy. For instance, Oruka's dismissal of ethnophilosophy as philosophy only in a 'debased' sense emphasizes that philosophy involves a critical approach. Although Wiredu accepts that oral tradition is a vital source in fashioning a modern African philosophy, he none the less believes that this should be subjected to critical assessment. Bell (1989: 364) asserts that philosophy engages in criticism to 'identify the biases of one's thought and to transcend or logically alter those thoughts for ones which more accurately reflect our natural and human world'. Philosophy thus acts as a catalyst for human understanding by providing new means of self-assessment.

All the conceptions of philosophy presented above are not mutually exclusive. For instance, there appears to be a close link between the view of philosophy as a conscious worldview and that of philosophy as a critical reflection. In addition, the concept of philosophy as a critical reflection does not imply that the issues criticized have no need of clarification or that they do not express a concern for love of knowledge.

Based on the above, this study recognizes all the conceptions of philosophy presented here as important, albeit in varying degrees. The conception of philosophy as clarification or analysis of concepts is especially important to this study, because of its concern with political philosophy. The terms used in political philosophy, such as 'justice', 'obligation', 'democracy', 'freedom', 'equality', 'liberty', and issues discussed such as 'what is a just society?', 'what are human rights?', need to be clarified in order to avoid confusion. For instance, when people refer to African leaders' subservience to foreign manipulation as neo-colonialism or to the tyranny of African leaders towards their subjects as neo-colonialism, it becomes difficult to understand what is meant without clarification.

The conceptions of philosophy most vital to this book, however, are those of philosophy as a conscious worldview and as a critical reflection. From these standpoints, philosophy is seen as performing a reactive role. The basis for embarking on this study is to evaluate the extent to which the ideas generated by creative writers, specifically Achebe and Ngugi, might help in promoting African self-understanding, with particular reference to the political situation on the continent. This inevitably means that their ideas are not presented as standing in no need of reassessment; instead, they will be critically assessed before being accepted, reformed or rejected, and it is on this basis that the claim of this study can be either validated or refuted. Ideas generated by creative writers might increase our understanding of the contemporary African political situation and help to show the way forward, but my conclusions should not be seen as definitive; they should, rather, act to further the critical tradition. After all, philosophy thrives on constant criticism and 'remains vigorous and healthy only if it is self-critical' (Raphael 1976: 7).

Literature

In a general sense, literature means 'any written expression or manifestation of thought – the products being considered as a collective body' (Poggioli 1963: 461). Under this umbrella, philosophical treatises, works of history, travel and adventure, essays on political, psychological, religious, social or even literary topics, books by scientists, biographies and autobiographies, and of course poetry, drama and prose are called literature.

The focus of this book, however, is on what is referred to as imaginative literature, defined as the attempt to present mankind and the environment via invented sayings and doings. This genre encompasses only poetry, drama and prose – short stories and novels.

Poetry operates through a marriage of high beauty of thought or language with artistic form. It provides a unique source of study and reflection and at its best enlarges experience. Maik Nwosu (1998: Preface) declared that the truly great poets known to him were 'those who in various ways have succeeded in effecting a marriage of the twin forms of beauty: the beauty that we sense and the beauty that sensitizes us and expands our horizons'. Joseph Brodsky claimed (in Carroll 1998: v): 'within a very short space a good poem covers enormous mental ground, and often, toward its finale, provides one with an epiphany or a revelation'. For Niyi Osundare (1983: 3–4), 'poetry is/a lifespring ... poetry/is/man/meaning/to/man'.

Poetry, whether written or oral, represents the highest type of artistic expression. It extracts and condenses language and emotion. In poetry, more than in drama and prose fiction, language plays a special role. This high concentration of meaning can render poetry inaccessible and obscure and restrict its audience.

Drama is a composition intended to be performed, and it is in this way that its full meaning is actualized. According to Marjorie Boulton (1960: 3), 'there is an enormous difference between a play and any other form of literature. A play is not really a piece of literature for reading. A true play is three-dimensional: it is literature that walks and talks before our eyes.' In drama the audience can see and hear the events as they unfold.

The success of a play consequently depends, in large measure, on its ability to carve out plots from the prevalent mode of the time so that an audience is able to recognize it, however altered. Henshaw (1956: 5) points out that 'dramatists have always known that the drama is one way in which they can "catch the conscience" of people. But this cannot be achieved if their audience does not understand the situations in their plays.' A good play for Chris Dunton (1992: 2) should conform to 'the broader context of social formation'. By this he means how 'plays relate to currents of thought, of ideological patterning, in contemporary ... society; how do they function as social production if and when they are performed; what do they do?'

From these disparate submissions emerges the conclusion that drama has great influence on life. The experience of taking part in a drama can greatly modify or deepen an actor's personal life; equally, the audience's appreciation of a situation, indeed of life itself, can be enhanced through drama.

Prose is a narrative, usually in ordinary spoken and written language with words arranged simply to make them more accessible to readers. The specific concern of this book is the novel. A novel depicts invented characters by utilizing invented sayings and doings (Mayhead 1965: 11). It can take many different forms: historical, psychological, romantic, sociological, political and so on. Here, attention is focused mainly on the political novel (represented by *Anthills* and *Petals*). The writer of such a novel, with the aid of imaginative creativity, renders an account of the nature of governance, authority, justice, equality, freedom and human rights, among other topics. The imaginative writer also attempts to account for the nature of the interactions or relationships existing among the constituents of a political culture. The novel can thus extend our understanding of life and of the many events happening in and around us.

In this way, the novel not only helps to shape our worldview, but also offers new means of reassessing accepted beliefs and ideas. The novel can provoke critical reflection, becoming a means of raising social consciousness and ultimately contributing to the task of achieving a better understanding of mankind and the world. Achebe (in Ezenwa-Ohaeto 1997: 263) sums up this point well: 'literature should make it possible for us, by observing the tragedies of fictional characters and fictional societies, to circumvent them; we should not have to go through the same thing once again'.

The affinity between philosophy and literature

Theoretical disciplines Essentially, philosophy and literature are theoretical disciplines. The interest of the philosopher is in ideas; by examining and clarifying ideas philosophy affects mankind and the world in a critical way. Socrates' insistence that an unexamined life is not worth living and his exhortation to man (*sic*) to know himself underscore the role of philosophy in helping to expand self-understanding. Moreover, in the cause of examining and clarifying ideas, a philosopher becomes something of a prophet, predicting future developments with remarkable insight and expressing new meanings in the search for true values (Mason 1982).

The concern of the imaginative writer is equally with ideas. By using words to invent characters, dialogue and plot, the imaginative writer can challenge traditional views as well as offer prophetic insights into human life. Achebe's *A Man of the People*, for instance, describes the events in Nigeria, after independence, that culminated in the country's first military coup; published two days after the actual coup, the novel ended prophetically with such a military coup. George Orwell's *Nineteen Eighty-Four*, written in 1948, predicts what mankind could do to itself and the world with increasingly sophisticated technology. Orwell's vision of future events corresponds in many important respects with what has been happening since the 1980s, for example the proliferation of nuclear weapons.

His Excellency, Sam, in Achebe's *Anthills* (1987) accurately portrays General Sani Abacha, the military head of state of Nigeria from 1993 to 1998. Like Abacha, he has an inordinate sense of power; his ambition to transform himself into a life-president is still unrealized at the time he meets his death in a manner shrouded in mystery. Ngugi, in an interview with Jane Wilkinson (1992: 130), asserts that the *gicaandi* artist in his novel *Devil on the Cross* is both a poet-singer as well as a prophet, because 'the singer, the poet, the man of words was often seen as a prophet ... who would know the truth and narrate the truth'. Okigbo's *Labyrinths* (poems prophesying war) also attest to his visionary ability. His prophecy about war in Nigeria came to pass; he was killed in the conflict he predicted. Some of his lines heralding the war read: 'So let the horn paw the air howling goodbye ... / O mother mother Earth, unbind me; let this be my last testament ... ' 'Path of Thunder' was indeed Okigbo's 'last testament' (Okigbo 1971: 71).

By using words to invent characters, dialogue and plot, the writer is less tied to fact and consequently has scope to comment on the facts either 'as they were or are, or as they are said to be or seem to be, or as they ought to be' (Aristotle 1965b: 69). Thus the ideas contained in creative works, if adequately utilized, can affect mankind and the world in a critical way. Writing on 'The Truth of Fiction', Achebe (1988: 95–6) opines that: 'Art [literature] is man's constant effort to create for himself a different order of reality from that which is given to him; an aspiration to provide himself with a second handle on existence through his imagination.' Philosophy and literature both bear testimony to the power of ideas in helping to shape mankind's self-understanding.

Moral influence In trying to shape mankind's ideas, both philosophy and literature exert moral influence on human behaviour. Ethics, a core branch of philosophy, is concerned with questions of human conduct and moral judgements (evaluations of conduct to establish whether it is good or bad, with a view to the attainment of the good life). Socrates went about stirring up the youths of his day by inquiring into the reasons for men's actions and pointing out the irrationality underlying many of their existing moral judgements. In this way he sought to point men to reason as the true standard for moral living. Plato endorses this moral guide by pointing men to wisdom, which reflects the eternal laws of the good. Aristotle locates the good life in the mean between extremes. For the Christian Church the moral life is one that is intimately connected to the being and character of God, seeing sacred scripture as containing commands concerning what is virtuous and what is vice and detailing the reward or punishment consequent upon each. Ethics thus acts as a reminder of the approbation that attends good deeds and of the adverse consequences of bad ones.

In the same vein, one reason why great works of literature are considered great is because of their moral stature (Mayhead 1965: 45). For instance, Amos Tutuola's *The Palm-wine Drunkard* and Achebe's *Things Fall Apart* have a high degree of moral interest, in that they tell us a great deal about some aspects of human life. The reader is led to see and evaluate the consequences of human excesses and to witness what happens when the order of things is subverted. A writer, through his or her art, can get the reader to feel actively involved in characters and events as if that reader is actually participating in them. Julian Mitchell calls this the process of 'entering into' an imaginary character, a unique way of extending our knowledge by enlarging our imaginative understanding of other human beings (Mitchell 1973: 22).

In *Things Fall Apart*, for example, Achebe transforms fear into a living force. The reader, perhaps, without sanctioning Okonkwo's action, is able to participate fully in the dominant emotions that propelled him to take part in the killing of Ikemefuna. In the end, the reader does not remain an outsider but an initiate who through the imaginative process of 'entering into' can no longer remain the same. This is what Mayhead (1965: 45) means when he states that 'anything that modifies a reader's ideas and feelings about his own and other people's lives has a moral effect upon him'. Mitchell (1973: 15) also endorses this position, noting that 'fiction has from earliest times been a means of moral instruction' because 'both in listening and reading our imaginations are extremely active, both creatively and critically'.

The imaginative writer is thus motivated by the kind of ethical concerns that engage the philosopher. For while ethics can instruct on how to live the good life, the reading of literature 'explains so much to us and affects radically the way we perceive the world thereafter' (Achebe 1988: 101).

Enlarging experience Both philosophy and literature enlarge our experience. By employing reason, philosophy tries to discover not only what is, but what ought to be. Plato's world of Forms is one such attempt. Others include philosophy's examination of issues such as: what is the chief good? Is life meaningful? Is the self a series of experiences and accidents, or is it a substance? What is the nature of the relationship between the universal and the particular? To what extent is memory reliable as a source of knowledge? Is man free? Was Judas's action free when it was written that the Son of Man would be betrayed? In trying to provide answers to these questions, philosophy helps to broaden mankind's experience and also assist in equipping humanity with an understanding of the meaning of life.

Similarly, the world to which literature exposes us is broader than anything personal experience can achieve. For instance, a reader going through Achebe's and Ngugi's novels is exposed to the conditions of modern Africa, especially the continent's political culture. This covers the pre-colonial days of Africa's proud warrior tribes; the European control of Africa under the guise of a civilizing mission and the subsequent subjugation and humiliation of the African; post-colonial freedom and sovereignty; and the betrayal of the independence dream. In effect, literature broadens our horizons by telling us things we would not otherwise have known about our existence. By reading Ngugi's novels, children born after the Mau Mau struggle of the 1950s will be able to identify meaningfully with that aspect of Kenya's past. Mayhead asserts:

> It has been the lot of the great imaginative writer, since what we know of the beginnings of literature, to see and face different aspects of this whole vast complexity we call human life, and to convey his interpretation of them as faithfully as possible to his audience ... And this is precisely why ... the reading of good literature can bring a man more closely into contact with the 'real world' than he could ever have been brought without a degree of personal experience for which the span of most lives is insufficient. (Mayhead 1965: 12)

Literature and philosophy thus enlarge mankind's experience by making readers conscious of a variety of ways of looking at life. A reader is made aware of things concerning humanity which are most likely to be of great relevance.

Human life Philosophy and literature are intimately concerned with human life. Philosophy embodies mankind's constant struggle to comprehend the myriad features of the world and to examine human progress. For Staniland (1979: 10), 'life is to the philosopher what the laboratory is to the scientist. The real test of a philosophical position is practical: how do things work out if we reform, modify or conserve our ideas in the way that the philosopher suggests?' In effect, philosophy is not about some abstract thing called life but about the day-to-day activities and problems that daily confront mankind.

Correspondingly, the imaginative writer 'in one way or another, is interested in people, in their variety, in their speech and behaviour, in their thoughts, feelings, and sensations' (Mayhead 1965: 14). By distilling his materials from his environment, an imaginative writer is able to create or re-create human life in such a way as to call into question mankind's basic assumptions and everything humanity has achieved. Ngugi, in an interview with Jane Wilkinson (1992: 131), asserts that as a writer he is basically interested in 'human relationships and the quality of human relationships and indeed the quality of human life', and as such he is interested 'in exploring all those social forces that prevent the realization of a more humane quality of human life and human relationship'. Philosophy and literature thus provide a rallying point for mankind in the effort to synthesize the multiple elements of human existence.

Language Philosophy and literature are united in their vigorous use of language. Beliefs, ideas, ideologies, culture, knowledge, experience, value and, of course, prejudice are acquired and conveyed through language. Words act as guides to the interpretation of social reality and, invariably, affect every aspect of a people's spiritual and material civilization and socio-political life. Depending on their positive or negative impact, words can shape people's ideas about themselves, their aspirations, conduct and learning abilities as well as portray them in a favourable or unfavourable light before others. Philosophical reasoning usually follows a method of conceptual analysis. This is important in determining the kind of knowledge philosophical inquiry yields. As such the careful use of language promotes clear thinking. It may have been in line with this that Eugen Rosenstock-Huessy (1963: 747) quotes William Ockham (Occam) as stating that 'entities should not be multiplied beyond necessity' (a proposition known as 'Occam's Razor'). By thinking more clearly we may be able to revive our society and change it for the better.

Similarly, literature helps to preserve the precision and vitality of language. By paying close attention to the linguistic environment, a writer is able to portray characters recognizable through their use of language. The choice of words a speaker employs depicts his or her disposition – favourable or unfavourable – towards the object of reference. When Mr Green in Achebe's *No Longer at Ease* explains Obi's accepting a bribe by saying 'the African is corrupt through and through', the word 'corrupt' conveys a negative disposition towards the African. Such an assessment, whether objective or not, is bound to affect other people's acceptance or rejection of the African. The fullest expression of mankind's personality lies in language – how people define themselves and how others define them through language. Achebe (in Wilkinson 1992: 49) asserts that writers 'must listen carefully and learn how people speak and convey it carefully'. He also (Achebe 1988: 91) cautions that 'when language is seriously interfered with, when it is disjoined from truth, be it from mere incompetence or

17

worse, from malice, horrors can descend ... on mankind'. Mayhead (1965: 14) also opines that the imaginative writer has a greater than ordinary interest in the possibilities of language because the language humans use is inextricably bound up with their lives.

In his story 'Running', David Njoku (2000) goes beyond the ordinary meaning of running as racing to explore its metaphysical sense as seeking escape from guilt. In the course of writing about people and their lives, a writer may sensitize us to the extent language affects, structures, shapes and interprets all aspects of human life; the extent to which language can be manipulated in favour or against an ideology, a person or even a whole people; the role of language in conditioning thought and perception and in identity formation; the extent colonial languages embody attitudes, referential meanings and perceptions that have greatly helped to distort the identity of Africans and their continent; how linguistic imbalances reflect real-life inequalities, inequities and ultimately suppress development; as well as describe and label new experiences that may become new vocabularies and part of reality.

Social functions Both philosophy and literature perform social functions. By employing criticism in the sense identified by Staniland, the philosopher is able to challenge and extend established traditions. The Socratic technique of interrogating our day-to-day actions and preconceptions is a vital tool of the philosopher. Socrates employed this technique to such an extent that he was accused of corrupting the Athenian youth of his day and was consequently put to death. Plato's emphasis on the ideal as the authentic reality changed mankind's worldview and led to the practice of regarding worldly things as unreal. Karl Marx, as stated earlier, insists that the new task for philosophers is to change the world. Philosophy thus serves as a vital tool for social reconstruction, thereby raising the social consciousness of mankind.

Equally, literature is a force that can be used for definite social purposes, acting as an instrument of revolution by challenging and compelling us to take a second look at things that we may hitherto have taken for granted. In *Petals*, Ngugi treats prostitution as a social problem resulting from far-reaching causes with deterministic implications rather than assuming that women go into it for various personal reasons. In *Anthills*, Achebe subverts the traditional prerogative of name giving by the man by imposing that task on Beatrice. Achebe insists that the issue of social consciousness is vital to literature, especially to an African writer. He states: 'An African creative writer who tries to avoid the big social and political issues of contemporary

Africa will end up being completely irrelevant.'[2] Even when literature functions purely as a means of entertainment it still

relaxes by exercising, bringing into play facilities of the mind that would otherwise lie dormant. It distracts, not by offering a cowardly escape from the business of living, but by making living fuller and more meaningful. Literature can take us out of the track of weary routine, by leading us to understand something of that whole vast body of human living in which our day-to-day concerns have their place. (Mayhead 1965: 9)

The reading of literature, then, provides a framework for articulating our daily experience, and becomes an instrument for the discovery of new ideas. It thus promotes our social consciousness by challenging our traditional standards. Achebe (1988: 103) puts it this way: ' ... fiction calls into full life our total range of imaginative faculties and gives us a heightened sense of our personal, social and human reality'. In this way, literature serves as a vital tool for social building and reconstruction. And like philosophy, it provides basic intellectual frameworks within which people can interpret, perceive and transform human experience (Oladipo 1993: 7).

Development Human beings are continuously striving to find new and better ways of improving their situation and managing their resources. For a society to progress, grow, advance, expand, change – in a word, develop – human resources are vital.

Philosophy and literature both have people and their world as the object of their consideration. Their primary concern is to give expression to human life in all its different aspects. The philosopher's interest in mankind, therefore, is not limited to a specific area. The various branches of philosophy (logic, metaphysics, ethics, epistemology, aesthetics), and its applications (philosophy of language, philosophy of science, philosophy of religion, philosophy of law, philosophy of social science and so on), attest to this.

In like manner, the concern of literature is mankind as a whole. The imaginative writer probes into the nature of mankind, human life, actions, progress, environment, limitations. Godwin Sogolo (1981: 113) quotes the Victorian novelist George Gissing as summing up the objectives of his work in this way: 'I mean to bring home to people the ghastly condition (material, mental and moral) of our poor classes, to show the hideous injustice of our whole system of society, to give light upon the plan of altering it, and, above all, to preach an enthusiasm for just and high ideals in this age of unmitigated egotism.' Joseph

Ukoyen (1993: 42) also asserts that 'literary activity adopts a holistic approach to the study of human character and personality'. Literature thus covers all facets of mankind. And like philosophy, it deepens and enhances human imagination, which in turn helps in the promotion of mankind's full development.

Universal essence Philosophy and literature attempt to depict the universal essence of mankind. Philosophy does not concern itself with whether, for instance, it is right or wrong for Mr A to steal but rather whether it is right or wrong for mankind to steal. Thus questions such as: what is right conduct? What is justice and fair play? How should power be exercised? are aimed at providing answers not directed at a particular person's actions but at humanity as a whole. Perhaps Kant's categorical imperative, that man should act only on that maxim that he can at the same time *will*, best summarizes this point.

Similarly, the imaginative writer, in depicting the human situation, usually concentrates on universal conflicts. For instance, Achebe's *Anthills* and Ngugi's *Petals* probe the nature of governance, power and the nature of interaction existing among the constituents of a political culture. Shakespeare's *Macbeth* is not necessarily about a particular Scottish man called Macbeth. Its application is to human life as a whole, in that it speaks to anyone in whatever society about the evil consequences of unbridled ambition and greed. Achebe, in his interview with Wilkinson (1992: 56), tells of how a white American boy, after reading *Things Fall Apart*, came to him and said: 'This Okonkwo is my father.' According to Mayhead (1965: 43): 'it [literature] can teach us about one another; and yet, at the same time as instructing us about one incidental difference which divides us, it can show us that we are fundamentally one'. Aristotle suggests that poetry is philosophical; its statements are of the nature of universals. The imaginative writer, by using invented characters, can thus portray life in general. By telling the story of particular individuals, the writer can say something of universal significance for mankind.

Perennial issues Philosophy and literature are also concerned with the perennial issues of mankind's existence. Philosophy is generally taken as beginning with the attempt to understand the basic stuff of all things. It embodies mankind's striving to apprehend and interpret the infinite. Is there a world beyond the mere physical? What are the ultimate meaning, value and purpose of human existence? What is the place of the divine in human life? Will this world ever pass away? If it does, what will replace it? Will mankind still be a part of the new formation? Will mankind ever cease to be? These are some of the perennial issues for which philosophy seeks to find answers. Literature also attempts to extend mankind's existence beyond the mere finite. By exploring the life of individual characters and events, the imaginative writer can probe such perennial issues as the meaning, value and purpose of human existence. Does mankind expect to live for ever? Who do humans think they are, and how do they relate to things and other humans? Are mankind's actions controlled by superior forces or governed by free will? To what extent can mankind interpret and understand reality? Does mankind have any relationship with the divine? If so, what is the place of mankind in the universe of the divine? Okigbo (1971: 53) wonders: 'But what does my divine rejoicing hold?' Perhaps Albert Salomon's observation (1957: 16) best sums up this point: 'The nature of the poet is a perennial one; there is the consistency of intent to interpret man's complex character, his relation to his fellow man, his living in the world, and his belonging to the universe of a divine and absolute meaning.'

Unrelated issues Philosophy and literature both probe the relation between things ordinarily not perceived as related. The philosopher, through sustained insight, can reconcile extreme concepts, such as appearance and reality, time and eternity, free will and determinism, freedom and responsibility. Kant, for instance, acted as a critical mediator between scepticism and dogmatism. He agreed with the empiricists that experience is the foundation of our knowledge, but pointed out that it does not follow that all knowledge arises out of experience.

The imaginative writer, also through sustained reflection, can relate things that are not normally considered connected. Jacqueline Costello and Amy Tucker (1989: 617) quote Percy Bysshe Shelley as proclaiming that it is the poet's art to make up fresh metaphors and word associations that express the 'unapprehended relations of things'. For them 'very often poets lead us to recognition of an abstract idea or emotion by using everyday words in unexpected ways' (ibid.). T. S. Eliot captures the image of the modern man in this line: 'men and bits of paper, whirled by the cold wind'.[3] By employing devices such as metaphor, simile and allegory, the writer can reconcile apparently opposing concepts. He or she is able to see the patterns of meaning in what ordinarily would seem an amorphous succession of episodes in the drama of life (Olapido 1993: 15). Mayhead (1965: 135) notes: 'It is the writer's imagination which catches at hitherto unperceived relations between things.' Thus contact with the work of a great writer can give us 'a completely new and refreshing sense of the world in which we live' (ibid.).

Boundary spanning Philosophy and literature broaden the horizons of society by operating outside standard laws and formulae. Philosophy does not limit itself to the past, nor to the present, but attempts to probe into what should be, the yet to come. It is, therefore, futuristic in outlook. Plato's 'Forms' and Kant's 'Noumena' are attempts to interpret reality beyond what is perceived.

Literature is also not limited to the past or the present, but includes things yet to be. Aristotle, as already noted, argues that poetry is more philosophical than history because it does not only account for things as they were or are, or as they are said to be or seem to be, but also as they *ought* to be. Ngugi's *Petals* ends with Karega's vision of cleansing the system of all the evils introduced through capitalism and instituting communism so that workers and peasants can fully enjoy the fruits of their creative labour. Achebe, in an interview with Kalu Ogbaa (1981: 4), asserts that writers write because they see a vision of the world better than what exists, a possibility of mankind rising higher than they have presently risen. For Leo Lowenthal (1961: xiii), 'the study of the history of the individual as portrayed in literature can tell us how we got here and, by so doing, enhance our ability to assess where we are going'.

Literature and philosophy are thus united in their ability to transcend the empirical realm and enter into a universe of the ideal. The philosopher and the imaginative writer, therefore, know that the universe of mankind is larger than the social process. Philosophy and literature are intimately connected in trying to provide a comprehensive worldview by examining the basic questions about mankind and the purpose(s) of existence. By so doing, they act as catalysts for human understanding by suggesting new ways of self-assessment. Staniland's (1979: 3) definition of philosophy as 'criticism of the ideas we live by' is also applicable to literature, just as Caute's observation (1978: x) that Sartre asserts that literature should be an irritant instead of a sedative, 'a catalyst provoking men to change the world in which they live and in so doing to change themselves', is true of philosophy.

Literature as political philosophy

The nature of political philosophy Political philosophy should be distinguished from political theory. Contemporary political philosophy lacks a settled nature (Plant 1998). It has traditionally often been used synonymously with the term political theory, which has, in its turn, been described as resembling a blank cheque which can variously denote a philosophy, an ideology or a science (Rathore 1976: 41). Its amorphous nature is such that L. S. Rathore (1975: 327) notes that one observer considers political theory as inseparable from thought; another holds that it is indistinguishable from philosophy; a third points out the need to separate it analytically from philosophy and ideology; while a fourth contends that it is the most accommodating of intellectual activity and, in effect, holds that thought, philosophy and ideology are specific forms of theory.

In order to avoid this confusion, it is necessary to limit philosophical theorizing on politics to political philosophy and the political scientist's theorizing to political theory. By delimiting the philosopher's concern to political philosophy and the scientist's to political theory, however, we are not making a case for a value-free political science theory.[4] Our purpose is simply to ensure that our discussion on political philosophy is not at any point mistaken for the activity of the political scientist in the attempt to secure a fact–value dichotomy political theory.

To obviate the possibility of any confusion, political theory is here taken to represent theorizing about society and the state undertaken by political scientists in the scientific sense of the term; it aims at explanation (Raphael 1976: 1–2). The political scientist tries to build up theories concerning society and government based on fact. Political philosophy, on the other hand, can be defined as a philosophical reflection on the ideal standards for society and government and their justification – which political institution will serve mankind the best? What criteria should be used to judge its ends, methods and achievements? What should be the ideal standard for society and government? What should be the nature of justice? Should it be central to political life? Should the citizen disobey the state if treated unjustly?

Given these and other related questions, political philosophers over the centuries have tried to justify one political institution as better than others. For instance, Plato's idea of an ideal political community is set out in his *Republic*. In it, the functions of the ruler and of the philosopher are fused. It is only through this means that the community can enjoy perfect justice, because the philosophic ruler, by virtue of his intellectual wisdom, will know what is good for the community. Aristotle, however, rejects Plato's ideal political community; he claims that the aristocratic form of government is the best. For Aristotle what is important is not a particular form of an ideal government but the relation between government and social order.

For Hobbes, to prevent man from going back to the condition of fear and brutishness that characterizes his state of nature, there is need for a legal-political community that is 'leviathan'. Locke locates the justification for a political society in the need to protect property (by which he means lives, liberty and estates), which may be jeopardized if each man is allowed to be the judge in a dispute.

Marx and Engels contend that material consideration is the basis for political systems. What are important in a society are the forces of production, and these are what determine what obtains in the political system of that society. As such, a dominantly capitalist society cannot offer man political freedom because of the conflict that is bound to exist between the class that controls the mode of production and the class that does not.

Political philosophers, therefore, attempt to set basic principles that will, for instance, 'justify a particular form of state, show that individuals have certain inalienable rights, or tell us how a society's material resources should be shared among its members. This usually involves analysing and interpreting ideas like freedom, justice, authority and democracy and then applying them in a critical way to the social and political institutions that currently exist' (Miller 1998: 500). This quotation exposes some essential features of political philosophy, among them the need for analysing and interpreting political ideas, here referred to as conceptual analysis or clarification, and a critical evaluation of these ideas. We will consider now each in turn.

Conceptual analysis or clarification Without unduly rehashing our previous discussion, there is still need for one or two inputs as well as a restatement of its decisive role in political philosophy. Arthur Ripstein (1997: 285) observes that conceptual analysis and clarification were central in the trends that shaped political philosophy in the first half of the twentieth century. Raphael (1976: 15) also notes that it is not hard to justify a purely conceptual treatment so far as political philosophy is concerned.

Basically, our appreciation of what is involved in conceptual analysis and clarification relies on understanding the terms employed in presenting political beliefs and general political principles. This is especially important since political concepts are essentially contestable – their meanings are mostly relative to a particular discourse. For instance, there are many variants of democracy. Aristotle employed the term to mean the rule of many in their narrow interest, differing from Abraham Lincoln's definition of it as government of the people, by the people and for the people. There is also a difference between liberal and communist democracy.

Clarification is a necessary condition for a belief to be retained or defended. This will not only make clear the exact intended definition but also show the logical relationship existing between the term and another. Raphael (ibid.: 12) refers to this function of showing the logical relationships whereby one concept implies or is implied by another as synthesis. For instance, the concept of leadership implies and is implied by the concept of discipleship. In this way, clarification invariably ends in improving our appreciation of concepts. Raphael, in fact, notes (ibid.: 12–17) that analysis, synthesis and improvements of concepts are three important related purposes in trying to clarify general political ideas.

In sum, conceptual clarification remains central to political philosophy if confusion is to be avoided in the presentation of political beliefs and general political principles.

Critical evaluation of beliefs This has also been discussed earlier. Our understanding of it is still the way Staniland employed it, to mean the giving of a rational, impartial and articulate justification for accepting a belief or for rejecting it. It remains only to show how critical evaluation applies to political beliefs. A basic task of political philosophers, as already noted, is to give a clear account of ideas such as Freedom, Justice, Authority, Right, Democracy. This, however, is not sufficient. For instance, to give an account of Justice, Plato came up with the idea of an ideal republic. In this republic, everything has a proper place and a proper function which lies behind the world of appearance; the task of the ruler and that of the philosopher is fused. This will guarantee perfect justice in the community. The philosopher-kings, by virtue of their intellectual wisdom, are the only ones equipped to create a society in harmony with the needs and aspirations of men. Justice in this context begins with each person locating and fitting into his station in life either as a tradesman, an auxiliary or a guardian. As such, the task of political philosophers extends to generating the ideas they evaluate.

Most of the ideas the political philosopher seeks to evaluate are value-related. This raises some critical issues for criticism itself. For instance, what criteria should be used in deciding what an ordered and just society will be in the case of two societies adopting different and incompatible ideas? What justifies a person in claiming authority to govern others, especially in a situation where other people with different ideologies are making the same claim? What, in short, is the guarantee that the critical evaluation of the political philosopher will represent what is right for man and society? These questions reveal some key features of the nature of political philosophy.

Political philosophy cannot possibly provide conclusive answers to the above questions. This inability, however, should not be regarded as a defect in political philosophy. It is enough that the political philosopher can show the consistency or inconsistency between sets of belief by elucidating their underlying implications. According to George Sabine (1939), 'the only absolutely general standard of rational criticism is the rule that a theory must not contain propositions that are mutually contradictory'.[5] Perhaps what is really important is that the political philosopher is able to show why some political arrangements count and others do not, since that is what underlies the activity of trying to justify a particular political arrangement as better than others. Raphael's observation perhaps best sums up this point. He noted (1976: 17) that the chief thing with which the study of political philosophy can equip us is not a final answer to problems but the habit of careful thought.

Let us now highlight some key features of the nature of political philosophy. First is the need for political philosophy to be critical, even at the expense of criticizing itself. Second, a good many of the questions posed in political philosophy are perennial in nature. Since the emergence of organized societies, mankind has tried, and continues to try, to arrive at the best political arrangement for collective existence. What should be the nature of the society and what kind of authority should it exercise over mankind? What should be the aim of a political institution? What is the proper place of individuals in society? How can they develop themselves and yet contribute to the achievement of the objectives of the state?

Further, the perennial questions also raise some issues as regards what should be the scope and status of political philosophy. Should the principles established by political philosophers be accorded a universal status? Or should they be regarded as reflecting the limited scope of the values and the assumptions of a given political community that has influenced a political philosopher?[6]

The questions also show a tendency towards justifying and criticizing existing and possible forms of political arrangement. A good deal of political philosophy can therefore be said to be normative.

Based on the foregoing, we can deduce that for a work to qualify as political philosophy it should conform to at least one of these features. One, it should attempt an analysis or clarification of political concepts. Two, it should attempt a critical evaluation of political beliefs, principles and general political arrangements. Three, it should attempt to generate political ideas. Finally, it should attempt to justify normative judgements about politics.

We will anchor our discussion on whether literature can be a political philosophy on the extent to which it is able to meet the above criteria. Our task now is to show that creative works can contain ideas that can be considered as political philosophy.

How literature can be a political philosophy Our discussion on political philosophy reveals its concern with the nature and wellbeing of mankind in society. To guarantee this wellbeing, it seeks justification and criticizes existing and possible forms of political arrangements, beliefs and practices. A good deal of political philosophy is, as such, taken to be normative. The political philosopher, then, does not merely evaluate political situations but also offers suggestions on what ought to be. It follows that political philosophers are to a great extent motivated because of their belief that a situation is bad. Hence political philosophy is usually the product of minds who have the sensitivity and the intellectual penetration to grasp political events in society and present them in such a way as to provoke critical reflection.

Equally, the literature of a society is usually the product of minds that have the intellectual capacity to capture its social phenomena – cultural, religious, economic as well as political. In this way, it can reveal much about the political arrangements, beliefs and practices in a place. Literature can, through the invention of characters and events, make serious observations on issues concerning our political life. Such issues include the relation between man and society, finding the best form of government for a people, investigating what is responsible for the way governments act, reviewing governmental effort in building a society where a fair opportunity will exist for everyone, articulating the political ideology that will be representative of a society, conceptualizing the role of opposition and identifying when opposition is justified, and stating the way power is, and should be, exercised.

But although literature may justify or criticize society, it does not merely passively record it (Lowenthal 1961: xv–xvi). The imaginative writer, through his or her work, can offer critical appraisal of the existing political situation and in this way mould or redirect society's actions, beliefs, ideals, values and ideas. Ideas contained in literature can influence people's perception about politics and the best means of effecting political change. It is in this light that Diamond (1989: 435) asserts that 'literature may affect the way people think about

27

politics, the way they perceive their political system, and the approach they embrace to the challenge of political change'. Michael Chapman (2003: 176) reminds us that 'it was a novel, Alan Paton's *Cry the Beloved Country* (1948), which perhaps more than any other "document" brought the South African racial problem to the attention of the world's conscience'.

In thus provoking people into assessing and criticizing their political situation, literature also performs a normative function. The imaginative writer through his or her work tries to set an ideal standard for society and the state. By exposing the political situation, a writer can directly or indirectly tell us what ought to be the case or what we ought to do. This way the work of an imaginative writer can serve the function of political philosophy. That is to say, imaginative works can contain ideas significant for understanding the political situation and invariably help to show a way forward. Some examples will help illustrate this.

Literary works as examples

No to colonialism: David Diop's 'The Vultures' In Africa, creative writers were at the vanguard in the fight for political liberation from colonial rule (Wautheir 1978: 144–79). For instance, most of the early poems written by Africans offer a criticism of the political situation under colonialism. These poems helped to mould people's perception and understanding of their political situation. David Diop's 'The Vultures' (1976) will serve as a good example.

The poem criticizes Africa's colonial experience – the hypocrisy of the European in controlling Africa under the guise of a civilizing mission. The role of Christian missionaries in converting Africa to a religion teaching men to be content with poverty is also shown as a calculated effort to favour tyrants by giving them passive slaves content with reciting the monotonous 'rhythm of the paternoster'. By the use of vivid images Diop not only questions the indignities and oppressive rule of those 'who knew all books' but also incites the African to despise and reject the condition of subjugation. Not even the colonial rulers' pride in the number of the skeletons of murdered Africans 'in the charnel-houses' nor their crass ravaging of the continent ('the desolate villages of Africa torn apart') will deter the African march towards independence: 'spring will be reborn under our bright steps'.

By using the image of the vulture, a carrion-eating scavenger, Diop casts doubt on the right of any nation or group of people to impose their reign on others. The poem also suggests that such a violent imposition – 'when civilisation kicked us in the face' – should be countered with 'hands instinct at the root with revolt'. The poem's denunciation of colonial rule and missionary antics, its identification with Africa and its oppression, and its provocative insistence on change, compel readers' intense involvement.

Don't civilize us, please: Sembene Ousmane's *God's Bits of Wood*

Sembene Ousmane, through his novels (1970, 1972, 1976), highlights and criticizes the social structure and politics in Senegal and throughout black Africa.[7] *God's Bits of Wood* is a case in point.

The novel deals with a significant event in the anti-colonial struggle in Africa: the strike on the Dakar–Niger railway in 1947–48. The novel portrays the kind of political atmosphere that breeds revolution – a society where injustice is entrenched. The white workers are paid more for working less while the black workers are paid less for working more; the health service and other things that might promote the wellbeing of mankind are reserved for a sector, in this case, the whites, while the blacks are ignored. Small wonder that Tiemoko's observation,

> we're the ones who do the work ... the same work the white men do. Why then should they be paid more? Because they are white? And when they are sick, why should they be taken care of while we and our families are left to starve? Because we are black? They tell us we have the same rights, but it is a lie, nothing but a lie! It does no good just to look at our pay slips and say that out wages are too small. If we want to live decently we must fight! (Ousmane 1970: 21)

is greeted with general approval for the strike. A revolution becomes the only weapon with which to fight for a decent life because 'it isn't those who are taken by force, put in chains and sold as slaves who are the real slaves; it is those who will accept it, morally and physically' (ibid.: 36). With this philosophy, the railway workers embarked on a strike that shook the whole country.

Through his novel, Ousmane calls attention to many socio-political problems caused by a nation imposing its system of government on another. Factors responsible for people's apathy towards government are highlighted. The effect of political instability in the life of an individual is exemplified by the case of the blind woman, Maimouna, whose son is crushed to death in the disturbance between the soldiers and the striking workers. The role of women is shown in their protest march from Thies to Dakar in support of the workers' strike. The management of the railway company is forced not only to negotiate on equal terms with the workers, but also to agree to meet their demands.

The eventual success of the workers underscores the role of the people in transforming their condition. Ousmane, in his prefatory note to the novel, observes: 'The men and women who, from the tenth of October, 1947, to the nineteenth of March, 1948, took part in this struggle for a better way of life owe nothing to anyone: neither to any "civilizing mission" nor to any parliament or parliamentarian. Their example was not in vain. Since then, Africa has made progress.' Although the urgent mission appears to be economic liberation, however, the political arrangement that makes it possible for a particular group of workers to be treated better than others is called into question. The strike raises questions that invite critical evaluation for both the colonized and the colonizer. Tiemoko notes (ibid.: 20) that 'this strike is like a school, for all of us'. It forces the workers to reflect on their status as a colonized people, especially when they realize what their collective forces could achieve – they experience 'a furtive astonishment at the forces they had set in motion' (ibid.: 53). Colonizers also have to rethink their myth of invincible power; 'how could such a small minority feel safe in the midst of these sullen masses?' (ibid.). The search for answers to these questions marks the beginning of a change in the status quo.

Dismantle apartheid now: Alex La Guma's *In the Fog of the Season's End* Some writers have also attempted to fictionalize the political situation in South Africa. Alex La Guma's (1972) *In the Fog of the Season's End* will serve as an example.[8] *In the Fog* deals with the struggle against apartheid in South Africa. Tekwane's arrest and torture in the novel's 'prologue' sets the stage for the fate that awaits dissidents. The government, instead of acting as an instrument for the pursuit of common good through reconciling the different interests of the people, becomes a tool for silencing unfavourable opposition. But in doing so, it fails to reckon with some characters who are sufficiently politically conscious to know that a government that deviates from its function of catering for the people's wellbeing is asking the people to abdicate their obligation to obey it.

Although the people are brutalized and perceived as 'things', their awareness that injustice must be countered with a revolution is unwavering, as demonstrated in Tekwane's refusal to cower before his oppressor. Instead, he tells his tormentor, 'you are going to torture me, maybe kill me. But that is the only way you and your people can rule us. You shoot and kill and torture because you cannot rule in any other way a people who rejects you' (ibid.: 6). His refusal to betray his ideals and beliefs, and his friends in the movement, reinforces his belief in the imperative of the struggle. His death, instead of acting to silence opposition, becomes the motive power for others to intensify the war against the regime.

In spite of the danger and the constant threat of state violence, Beukes remains undeterred in his political activism to free South Africa from the shackles of the apartheid regime. He tells us at the end of the novel that the war being waged by some of his friends against the regime 'is only the tip of an iceberg of resentment against an ignoble regime' (ibid.: 180). The reader is left to imagine a situation where there will be no peace in South Africa until the oppressive political situation that makes one person an oppressor and another an oppressed is revoked.

That the novel raised some disturbing political issues is not in doubt: it was proscribed in South Africa. This is evidence enough that the novel must have provoked people to the need to create a new world outside apartheid.

Post-independence – is it any better? Ayi Kwei Armah's *The Beautyful Ones are Not Yet Born*

Ayi Kwei Armah's novels have been seen by some scholars as representing a vision of society through their concern with the present socio-political chaos in Africa.[9] *The Beautyful Ones are Not Yet Born* will satisfy our purpose. In the novel Armah moves beyond the ills of colonialism to offer a biting analysis of the problems besetting post-independence Ghana. Armah provokes a critical examination of Ghanaian society, especially its political leaders, whose corrupt practices hinder any meaningful development in society. The leaders' interpretation of how power should be exercised is to engage in misappropriation of public funds, nepotism, massive bribery, graft and complete disregard for public wellbeing. And since the ills are perpetuated by 'the sons of the nation', there is no easy scapegoat and as such 'if the old stories aroused any anger, there was nowhere for it to go' (Armah 1969: 10). Even the Man, in spite of his moral rectitude, could not stop this pervasive corruption. The military moves in, with its usual sanctimonious attitude, to sanitize the country. Koomson and his corrupt party men are removed from power. Predictably, this fails to check the corruption in the society. Instead, it is like replacing one gang of robbers with another as the following passage taken from a scene after the coup reveals:

In the life of the nation itself, maybe nothing really new would happen. New men would take into their hands the power to steal the nation's riches and to use it for their own satisfaction. New people would use the country's power to get rid of men and women who talked a language that did not flatter them. That would only be a continuation of the Ghanaian way of life. The flatterers with their new white Mercedes cars would have to find ways of burying old words. For those who had come directly against the old power, there would be much happiness. But for the nation itself there would only be a change of embezzlers and a change of the hunters and the hunted. (ibid.: 162)

The reader is left to wonder if the problem is with the form of government or the complete disregard of the leaders to abide by the principles of responsiveness and accountability in the discharge of their duties.

Stop the fakes: Wole Soyinka's *The Trials of Brother Jero* Most Nigerian writers have also provoked critical evaluation of the political situation in Nigeria specifically and Africa in general. The works of Wole Soyinka and a more recent writer, Maik Nwosu, illustrate this concern.

Soyinka's works deal with such political issues (Adeniran 1994; Ikiddeh 1986). We will, however, limit our discussion to *The Trials of Brother Jero*. In this play, Soyinka captures not just the dangers posed by fake religious leaders to ordinary citizens but, more importantly, the effect of this fakery on the country's political leadership. The lack of focus and greed for power of political leaders are revealed through Member of Parliament's gullibility concerning Brother Jero's antics. He readily accepts Jero's prophecy that he will become 'Minister of War', which 'would be the most powerful position in the land' (Soyinka 1981: 41). And when Jero runs away from one of his disenchanted church members, Chume, Member interprets it as the miraculous disappearance of a true man of God. He takes off his shoes and sits to await his return, for 'perhaps he has gone to learn more about this ministerial post' (ibid.: 43).

Trials invites reflection on the dangers posed to society if a leader's mind, thoughts and actions can easily be controlled by a fake beach prophet. The proliferation of churches and the increase in crime make this a particularly incisive play. The function religion played in perpetuating colonial oppression is still part of recent history. The play thus holds a warning for leaders who would allow themselves to be manipulated into using religion as a base for their hidden nefarious

32

agenda. The reader is alerted to such charlatans, knowing that such people will never make good leaders.

See the people's misrepresentatives: Maik Nwosu's 'The Honourable Fartheads' Maik Nwosu's short story, 'The Honourable Fartheads' (Nwosu 1997), is a commentary on the corrupt practices of Members of Parliament who do not understand the concept of responsive and accountable government nor accept the need to act as the people's representatives.

Instead they see their positions as a means of engaging in petty tribal and sectional wrangling, using words as a replacement for action, intimidating political opponents, enriching themselves and perpetuating their grip on power. The only time the 'Honourables' are united – 'the usual division along party or faction lines had miraculously disappeared' – is when 'motions concerning the welfare of the lawmakers' are proposed (ibid.: 81).

This can, of course, be likened to political happenings in Nigeria, with special emphasis on the National Assembly, since independence. The internal wrangling in both the Senate and the House of Representatives at the expense of the bill they are supposed to be deliberating on and passing into law, and the ₦3.5 million furniture allowance saga in a country where some workers do not receive up to ₦5,000 as minimum wage, are both good examples of such practice.

Beyond cataloguing the ills in the political system, 'The Honourable Fartheads' also points to a new direction. Ime Uduak, the representative of the people of the backwater of Kali district, remembers his constituency only after six years, when his scheming brain reminds him of the need to build his political base in readiness for his intended gubernatorial race. He is, however, not prepared for the kind of reception that awaits him from his people. They completely shun his overture for a 'new covenant' and resolutely reject his 'heavy-weight briefcase bursting with currency notes' (ibid.). There cannot be a more explicit way of saying that they will not vote for him again.

'The Honourable Fartheads', therefore, makes the point that the people have a great responsibility in transforming their political situation by checking their leaders' excesses. The action of the Kali people can encourage readers to take up the challenge and the task of shaping their society. In this way, the story can contribute in creating the ideal society desired by the writer.

The above illustrations serve as evidence that the imaginative writer can assume the role of the political philosopher by engaging in critical evaluation of our existing and possible forms of political arrangements, beliefs and practices, helping our understanding of political concepts and justifying normative judgements about politics. The works of imaginative writers – literature – contain ideas significant for our understanding of our political situation and as such could be studied as political philosophy. What remains now is to demonstrate that the creative works of Achebe and Ngugi, the prime focus of this book, also meet this criterion.

THREE

Chinua Achebe and Ngugi wa Thiong'o as political thinkers

Chinua Achebe: a brief introduction

Nigerian teacher, novelist, essayist, social transformer and poet, Chinua Achebe was positioned at the crossroads of history, the intersection between the Igbo tradition and the colonial structure. He was provoked into becoming a writer by the desire to tell the story of Africa 'from the inside' as opposed to the misrepresentations of European writers, notably Joseph Conrad (*The Heart of Darkness*) and Joyce Cary (*Mister Johnson*).

Chinua Achebe was born to Isaiah and Janet Achebe on 16 November 1930 in Ogidi, near Onitsha, in south-eastern Nigeria. At that time Nigeria was under British rule, which ended in 1960. Achebe's father was a church teacher and Achebe was brought up in the parsonage of the church missionary society; he began to learn English at about the age of eight. He attended the Government College at Umuahia, then proceeded in 1948 to the new University College, Ibadan, with a scholarship to study medicine. Convinced after one year that he was in the wrong discipline, he switched to English literature, religious studies and history. This decision cost him his scholarship.

After graduating in 1953, Achebe taught for a year before joining the Nigerian Broadcasting Corporation in 1954, serving as director of the Voice of Nigeria from 1961 to 1966. After the Nigerian civil war, Achebe became a research fellow at the University of Nigeria in 1970 and in 1973 a professor of English. He was the head of department for the 1979/80 academic session, and became the editor of *Okike*, a journal that published new Nigerian writers, in 1971.

He retired from the university at the end of 1981 and was appointed professor emeritus in 1985. He was elected president-general of Ogidi Town Union in 1986. In the same year, he ended his four-year stint as president of the Association of Nigerian Authors, relinquished the position of editor of *Okike* and was appointed pro-chancellor of the Anambra State University of Technology, Enugu. In 1987 he was appointed honorary life vice-president of the Onitsha Chamber of Commerce. Achebe married Christie Chinwe

Okoli in 1961 and they have four children. He has worked at Bard College since 1990.

Achebe's writing career began with some short stories he published as a student in the *University Herald*. It was with *Things Fall Apart* that Achebe rose to fame. The book has sold millions of copies worldwide and has been translated into at least forty-five languages.

His other major works include: *No Longer at Ease*, 1960; *Arrow of God*, 1964; *Anthills of the Savannah*, 1987; and volumes of poetry and essays.

Achebe's pre-independence novels offer invaluable insight into the traditional life, and events from colonialism with their burdens, lessons and challenges to the moulding of an African identity. His post-independence works reflect his direct experience and examine defining political events in modern African history: independence and subsequent disillusionment leading (in Nigeria at least) to civil war and the entrenchment of military rule. They also express faith in the potential of the African peoples and suggestions concerning their future.

Achebe has inspired many generations of African writers. He writes extraordinarily well: his control of the pace of his stories, his arrangement of facts, effective use of suspense, the complete absence of contrivance, the social commitment informing his novels, his creation of a new form of English to express the African experience, his economy of words, are all attributes of a technically skilled novelist, a born artist.

Achebe has received honorary doctorates from more than thirty colleges and universities, many prizes and awards, including the Commonwealth Poetry Prize, 1974; Lotus Award for Afro-Asian Writers, 1975; the Nigerian National Order of Merit and the Order of the Federal Republic, 1979; Campion Medal, 1996 and First National Creativity Award, 1999.

Ngugi wa Thiong'o: a brief introduction

Ngugi, Kenyan novelist, teacher, playwright, essayist and political thinker, is considered the foremost writer among East African writers in English to emerge after Kenya's independence in 1963. His works provide the strongest links with Kenya's political past and also cover the four major stages in the development of modern African writing in English: imperialist incursion into Africa; the entrenchment of colonial rule and foreign culture and the beginnings of the anti-imperialist movement; revolt against imperialism and colonialism; and the post-independence period of disappointment. He was among the first writers to introduce a new order – the skilful manipulation of group action to effect a reversal of odds by the use of revolutionary action – to the African literary scene. The common people are his fundamental interest and their wellbeing his primary goal. He is currently Professor of English and Comparative Literature and the director of the International Center for Writing and Translation at the University of California.

A member of the Gikuyu ethnic group, Ngugi was born in Limuru on the edge of the Rift Valley, near Kamiriithu, in 1938. After attending a mission-run school at Kamaandura in Limuru, Karinga School in Maanguu, he became the only student from the whole of Limuru to get into the prestigious Alliance High School in 1955. When Ngugi went up to Makerere University College in Kampala (Uganda) in 1959, the syllabus and critical approach adopted by the English department were based on acknowledged Western classics and did not reflect emergent African literatures and local cultures, but at Leeds University (where he went to pursue graduate studies in 1964), his critical interaction with eminent socialist scholars and his reading of Frantz Fanon's *The Wretched of the Earth* and Robert Tressell's *The Ragged Trousered Philanthropists* reoriented him and turned him into a socialist.

Ngugi's socialism is reflected in his total identification with the masses, with the peasant class. He is convinced that a writer should write for the people, and he writes in a language that will allow him to communicate with peasants and workers in Africa. After the publication of *Petals of Blood* in 1977, Ngugi abandoned the English language as a vehicle for his plays, novels and short stories. His novels *Caitaani Mutharaba-ini (Devil on the Cross)*, and *Matigari*; his plays *Ngaahika Ndenda (I Will Marry When I Want)*, and *Maitu Njugira* and his children's books are written in Gikuyu.

On 31 December 1977 the Kenyan regime banned *Ngaahika Ndenda*, arrested Ngugi and put him in a maximum security prison, which became his home until 12 December 1978. On 25 February 1982 the Kenyan regime again stopped the rehearsals of his play *Maitu Njugira* after ten rehearsals. This eventually led to his being banned from teaching at the University of Nairobi; he went into exile.

Ngugi is perhaps the first African writer profoundly to articulate the paradox of African writers narrating and expressing themselves in the language of the colonialist, which embodies categories, biases and values that denigrate the African and against which the African writer must consciously and systematically work. Ngugi meets this challenge by bridging the gap between theorizing about making the ordinary people understand their situation and effect change and helping them to do so on a practical level. He understands that the real task facing a writer, to paraphrase Marx, is not merely to interpret the world but to change it. His restlessness in the presence of injustice, no matter how subtle it might appear, will reverberate in the conscience of both the just and the unjust.

Political thinkers

To provide a theoretical basis for judging Achebe and Ngugi's works as political philosophy necessitates providing a politico-ideological context that justifies this thesis. This chapter will show who the most influencial political thinkers are; and then attempt to establish whether Achebe and Ngugi can be considered alongside them. Some leading figures who have made substantial contributions to political thought and at the same time represent the most different significant approaches to political thinking are Plato, Aristotle, Machiavelli, Hobbes, Locke, Marx and Gandhi.

Only the ideal is good enough: Plato's *Republic* Plato is generally taken to be the first Greek philosopher to articulate, in an organized form, how a society should be arranged for the optimum realization of man's wellbeing (Plato 1941).

The *Republic* begins with an account of justice. Indeed, its thrust is to answer the question, 'what does Justice mean, and how can it be realized in human society?' (ibid.: 1). To understand Plato's notion of Justice properly and to apprehend his entire philosophy, is to appreciate his belief system: there is an ideal order, where everything has a proper place and a proper function, lying behind the world of appearance. A just society, one where every element performs its proper task, is for Plato the summit of political accomplishment.

But how can this be brought about? Plato conceives of man as made up of three elements – the appetite, spirit or soul, and reason – although one element will always predominate. Likewise, society consists of three classes of people, corresponding to the three elements in man: the tradesman, the lowest class, in which the appetite predominates; the auxiliary, the middle class, in which the spirit predominates; and the Guardian, the highest class, in which reason is predominant. Justice in the state depends upon the three classes performing distinct functions: the Guardian, deliberation and governance; the auxiliary, executive; and the tradesman, production. To enable these classes to master their different social functions and perform them rightly, education is all-important.

Plato also recognized that it is not automatic that the Guardian class will produce sons like them. It is none the less imperative for the ideal republic that virtuous rule endures. To ensure that the quality of the Guardian class is not compromised, Plato designs for it an elaborate intensive programme of education. The ideal state can come into being only if the 'philosophic statesman can be produced and educated and given a free hand to remould society' (ibid.: 256).

This system of education can be divided into stages. The elementary stage, which goes on until the age of eighteen, exposes young pupils to an awareness of reality and true knowledge. The survivors move on to the second stage, which involves military training and more rational inquiry. This lasts till the age of twenty. Those who succeed will form the auxiliary class, while those who show real competence move on to the third stage, devoted to profound intellectual pursuits. Here, initiates acquire true knowledge. To round off his education, the philosopher-king will undergo apprenticeship from thirty-five to fifty, when the best will reach the vision of the Good and be ready to direct the affairs of the state.

In this highly regimented, formalized and controlled system of education, it appears that Plato made no allowances for individual creativity, originality and initiative. Another interpretation, however (which could be what Plato is interested in) may be to show the benefit that awaits a society if people are encouraged to discover their natural inclinations and to follow them instead of dissipating energy in areas they cannot handle.

Plato also prescribed a system of communism regarding wives and property for his ideal state. The first ensures that rulers devote themselves fully to their civic duties, from which family responsibilities and attachments might prove a distraction. The second safeguards the aims of the state from personal ambition, selfishness and greed, which the possession of private property is likely to generate in rulers.

The *Republic* also contains an examination of various types of constitution. Plato attempts to delineate the process of decline in society and in the soul; as a corollary he shows the process of the degeneration of the just man into an unjust one, a decline starting from the fall of the ideal state and ending in despotism – with an absolute, unconstitutional ruler, a 'tyrant'. Plato considers despotism the lowest form of constitutional degeneration the state can experience, and the despotic man as a tyrant, as a ruler who loves power for its own sake and is ruled by ambition, fear and greed instead of reason and humanity. Under this system, opposition is silenced and the rulers surround themselves with scoundrels, while citizens are left defenceless and impoverished. Plato's dislike for forms of government such as aristocracy, oligarchy, democracy or tyranny is that they are ruled not by reason and justice but rather by appetite and whim.

Before criticizing Plato's ideal republic it is important to understand the background that shaped his thinking. Plato's vision of the political community is a reaction against the social disintegration taking place in his beloved Athens. His appeal to reason, to the Forms as the only authentic reality, has at its source a desire for a secure political community where justice can reign supreme, as opposed to the unjust life that characterized political affairs in his day. He sees social disorder as inevitable in a society not governed by reason. Hence his insistence on philosopher-kings, because they are the only ones who can create a society in harmony with the needs and aspirations of men.

The ideal republic and its philosophic rulers are more than an attempt to bring back the political order that existed in the Athenian city-state, especially under Cleisthenes. Robert Nisbet (1982: 8) notes that Plato's 'political philosophy is a blend of rigorous social nihilism and political affirmation'. Plato's interest extends to all influences that undermine political unity and in how best to eliminate them. In this way, his ideal political community with its non-existent kinship ties, a repudiation of anarchic individualism and a complete rejection of capitalism or any system that sanctions unchecked private property, is novel. Plato's mission is to propose a political community founded on justice that will guarantee freedom for the individual to fulfil his potential.

Plato's notion of freedom, however, is not completely 'free'. It is unlikely that an individual will be allowed to follow a path that threatens the set goal of the political community. For Plato, the survival of the political community is dependent on the education given to individuals to predispose them to a certain function, action, mental and moral attitude. It is this total control of all spheres of man's life that will bring about a just community.

Karl Popper criticized this rigid, close monitoring by the state in his book *The Open Society and Its Enemies*, seeing Plato's presentation as anti-democratic and the placing of the society above the individual as characteristic of a closed society. In Popper's view, Plato is an enemy of what is best in human civilization: an open society. But Popper and Plato lived in different worlds and applying modern standards to Plato's ancient times may not serve the purpose of critical reflection well; better to identify political issues raised by Plato's ideal state and develop our political thoughts on them. These issues include: what should be the true aim of the state? What should be the proper place of the individual in society? What is the best means by which the individual can develop himself and still contribute to the achievement of the objectives of the state? What kind of disposition and structure can provide and sustain justice in society? What is justice? In short, what is the ideal form of government?

Plato articulated some of the perennial issues of political philosophy. Francis Macdonald Cornford credits Plato with the foresight that enabled him to identify the ultimate problem of politics, one that confronts every age: 'How can the state be so ordered as to place effective control in the hands of men who understand that you cannot make either an individual or a society happy by making them richer or more powerful than their neighbours?' (Plato 1941: xxix). This inevitably brings 9/11, the terrorist attack on America, to mind. Alan Ryan's summary of the main thrust of Plato's argument in the *Republic* identifies two tasks: 'one to demonstrate that it is always better to suffer injustice than to commit it, the other to show that a city ruled by philosopher-kings would be happy, stable, and possible to create' (Ryan 1998: 368).

Let's establish the right balance: Aristotle's *Politics* In *Politics*, Aristotle sets down the conditions for the arrangement of the state so as to ensure the happiness of its citizens. He begins his political theorizing by accounting for the natural basis of society. For him, 'man is by nature a political animal'[1] and cannot live an isolated, self-sufficing life. A political community consists of different sorts of people, performing, as sailors have to perform, tasks towards a common object, which is safety in navigation: 'One citizen differs from another, but the salvation of the community is the common business of them all' (quoted in Ayer 1946: 161). The individual is as such a member of state and the state is by nature prior to the individual or the family. The state comes into existence 'when several villages are united in a single community, perfect and large enough to be nearly or quite self-sufficing' (ibid.: 158). And, of course, the state exists for the sake of a good life.

For Aristotle, the good life can be lived only in a city. And since the supreme good is to achieve the good life, securing the good life for the whole citizenry is better than securing it for an individual, for no one is self-sufficient. Besides, life in a city is part of the 'normal nature' of man, which distinguishes him from beasts. He sees a man who is unable to live in society, or who has no need because he is sufficient for himself, as either a beast or a god (ibid.).

The main purpose of the state is justice, seen as the 'bond of men in states', and its administration as 'the principle of order in political society' (ibid.: 159). But this can be effective only through laws. Aristotle recognizes that it is not possible that all citizens can be good, even in the good state. It will therefore be dangerous to allow a mere human individual to decide what will constitute justice in the city. Aristotle sees revolution as inevitable where government is not founded upon justice. That is, political changes take place as a result of dissatisfaction with the state of things.

Aristotle distinguishes between two types of rule, one for the sake of the rulers (despotic); and another for the sake of the ruled (free government) (ibid.: 164). A good ruler is one who has learned how to obey. This implies that one must be a subject before becoming a ruler. Indeed, the special characteristic of the citizen is that he takes part in the administration of justice, and in offices according to constitutional principle. The education of the governors and the governed must thus be the same and also different. It is the duty of the legislator to see that both the rulers and the ruled perform their duties in such a way as to maintain the perfect life. It is the law then, and not man, that can guarantee justice in the city. A well-run political community is based on laws and not men. Aristotle condemns tyrannies, oligarchies and unconstitutional democracies as government by self-interest rather than law, regarding them as unlikely to make the good life possible. He favours the law-governed polis, whether it is a monarchy, an aristocracy or a constitutional democracy.

Thus, far from advocating an ideal state as Plato did, Aristotle's primary concern is with finding the right balance between government and social order. He wants to ensure that the political arrangement is such that citizens and legitimate associations can achieve their ideal life without intimidation from whatever form of government is in existence. His interest in ensuring that differences are upheld naturally leads him to reject Plato's unified political community, whether in terms of total control of citizens' actions, functions, mental and moral lives; or as an expression of common ownership of property and wives for the Guardian class. Instead of the good Plato envisaged would come from this political arrangement, Aristotle sees it as most likely to result in the political death of a state. For instance, common ownership would translate to a loose notion of responsibility whereby what is commonly owned could easily be neglected by all. But what Aristotle wants to preserve most is the freedom of other communities within the political order, given the totalitarian nature of the political community. For Aristotle, Plato's social unity, far from leading to a better political community, will degenerate into a totalitarian society.

Alan Ryan (1998: 372) asserts that Aristotle's permanent legacy is 'the defence of politics against critics who wanted to smooth over social conflict and to tidy up the world by handing over absolute power to some superior person or persons'. For the political community to realize its highest good it is important that legitimate interests, however diverse, be encouraged. It is the duty of those who govern to harmonize these differences to achieve a common good. 'A state exists for the sake of a good life, and not for the sake of life only' (quoted in Ayer 1946: 159).

Gain the whole world: Machiavelli's *The Prince*: The credit for using the word 'state' in its political sense, beginning another era in political philosophy – the age of modern political philosophers – is usually given to Machiavelli. His most noted contribution to political thought is contained in *The Prince*, in which he documents his advice to rulers on how to manage state affairs.

Machiavelli believes that it is necessary for rulers to use two methods of fighting, one by law, which is that of men; and the other by force, which is the method of beasts. The prince must be able to imitate the fox and the lion so as to be able to recognize traps and be brave enough to frighten wolves. As such, 'a prudent ruler ought not to keep faith when by so doing it would be against his interest'.[2] It is also important for the ruler to be a 'great feigner and dissembler' to enable him to hide his cunning motives. A ruler should seem 'merciful, faithful, humane, sincere, religious' but must have a mind so disposed that when it is needful to be otherwise he will be able to adopt opposite qualities (Ayer 1946: 171). The Prince should aim to conquer and maintain the state through whatever means. He should have no qualms about killing those who harbour envy and evil passions against him. In short, rulers must calculate and their philosophy should be 'the end justifies the means'; there should be clear separation between private and public morality.

It would be a mistake to dismiss Machiavelli's political thought as unethical based on his advice to rulers. Machiavelli is reacting to the experience of his time that 'shows those princes to have done great things who have had little regard for good faith, and have been able by astuteness to confuse men's brains, and who have ultimately overcome those who have made loyalty their foundation' (ibid.: 170). His political vision, then, comes of a careful study of man. His advice to rulers to break their faith whenever it suits them is based on the

43

fact that men are as bad as, and consequently would not observe their faith with, their rulers. The advice for rulers to appear to possess mercy, faith, integrity, humanity and religion is likewise because 'men in general judge more by the eyes than by the hands, for every one can see, but very few have to feel' (ibid.: 171). Machiavelli's concern seems to be to ground the ruler in the practical facts of his position. Alan Ryan observes:

> the reason why Machiavelli is often thought of as a 'post-christian' philosopher is that he took what one might call the commonsensical view that the answer to Christ's question, 'what shall it profit a man if he gain the whole world and lose his own soul?' is that he would gain the whole world. That is, a man whose primary aim was to preserve his own moral innocence had no business in politics. (Ryan 1998: 374)

No matter how much we may want to disagree with Machiavelli, the political events of our present generation would seem to endorse his view that politics and morality are fundamentally incompatible.

Maximize control: Hobbes's *Leviathan* Thomas Hobbes is often acknowledged as 'the first writer to articulate the modern view of the state' and his *Leviathan* is seen by many, as by Ryan, as 'the greatest work of political theory written in the English language' (ibid.: 377–8). The age of modern political philosophers is often seen as having begun either with Machiavelli or Hobbes.

Hobbes began his political theorizing by trying to account for how mankind evolved from existing in the state of nature to living in a civil society. He rejected the Aristotelian conception of mankind as political animals, complaining that such a conception is based on 'too slight contemplation of human nature'.[3] For him the 'original of all great and lasting societies consisted not in the mutual good will men had towards each other, but in the mutual fear they had of each other' (quoted in Ayer 1946: 176). In the state of nature, mankind is utterly lawless and grasping and will do anything to protect 'only' its interests. Life in this state is solitary, poor, nasty, brutish and short. Without any law or a strong ruler to set limits, mankind is continually at war with itself and life is constantly exposed to fear and the danger of violent death. It is to overcome this state that mankind, being rational animals, will come to the realization of the need for rational self-preservation.

Hobbes notes nineteen laws of nature, rules a reasonable man will follow in pursuing his own advantage. He defines (ibid.: 181) the law of nature as 'the dictate of right reason, conversant about those things which are either to be done or omitted for the constant preservation of life and members, as much as in us lies'. The first and fundamental law of nature is to seek peace, since, in its absence war will prevail. The second requires us willingly to transfer or relinquish some certain rights to others, given that they are willing to do the same. That is, we should be willing to enter into a social contract, since the state where everyone can retain his or her right to all things invariably results in war, since such an act is against the reason of peace. Furthermore, the third law of nature enjoins men to abide by the contracts they enter into: 'he that is tied by contract is trusted (for faith only is the bond of contracts)' (ibid.: 182).

The laws of nature, however, cannot achieve their desired end without sanctions. It is for this that men agree to 'the mutual transferring of right'. Hence the desire to minimize the risks of social warfare that is his lot in the state of nature will compel every man to subject his will to some other one, to wit (ibid.: 185), 'either man or council, that whatsoever his will is in those things which are necessary to the common peace, it be received for the wills of all men in general, and of every one in particular'. It is this union that becomes a civil society or a city. Hobbes defines a city as: 'one person, whose will, by the compact of many men, is to be received for the will of them all; so as he may use all the power and faculties of each particular person, to the maintenance of peace, and for common defence' (ibid.: 186). Society and sovereign come into existence together as a result of the covenant.

There are two aspects of the social contract. First, the people agree among themselves to give up their rights. Second, they authorize a person or assembly of men to rule over them. In other words, the sovereign authority is not part of the agreement. Also the form of constitution, monarchic, democratic or aristocratic, established by the covenant is not important. What is necessary is that the sovereign's power should be entire, absolute and indivisible. It is the sovereign who determines what is done or not to be done for the common good.

Hobbes dislikes decentralization, whether of power or of corporate freedom to the Church. He sees division of any kind as likely to lead to a divided sovereignty within the state, which will inevitably result in political instability in society. For order to be maintained in society, authority must be centred in the state. In Hobbes, there are no transcendental moral laws; instead, the sovereign is above the law.

Hobbes's social contract appears to take a lot of things for granted, chief among them his supposition that human understanding will compel men to see the need to leave the state of nature. Secondly, there is his assumption that all men will come to the realization of the need to transfer their rights at the same time. But to dwell on these shortcomings is to neglect Hobbes's main preoccupation, which is to justify the need for a sovereign with absolute legal authority. Like Plato, Hobbes was reacting to the social disintegration in his society. He wrote the *Leviathan* at a time when England was going through severe internal crisis. There was the acrimony between the King and Parliament over who should exercise supreme authority. There was bloody civil war between the followers of the Stuarts and Cromwell's Puritans. The public beheading of Charles I took place during this period. The unprecedented robbing, pillaging, looting and burning that were daily happenings at this time all no doubt helped shape Hobbes's political vision; he sees these happenings as the kind of thing that could occur in a natural state of man. To stop man from returning to this ugly state of his being, there is need for an absolute sovereign with such overwhelming power as to contain civil wars, crimes and insurrections, and to suppress man's natural egoistic tendency, which could destroy the political order. The 'covenant' that brings the sovereign into power offers the only logical escape from the wretched life that was man's lot in the state of nature. Grant (1988: 706) credits Hobbes with pointing to a profound truth: 'in the last resort, authority derives not from the sovereign, still less from anything outside society, but from the subject himself, even if he is, so to speak, coerced by necessity into his act of authorisation'.

Hence, the rigid over-centralization one finds in Hobbes notwith-standing, it is a mistake to read his position as merely vesting power in the sovereign to the point of intimidating the individual. His concern is rather with creating an environment where individuals can realize their highest potential. Both his premise that the war of all against all is responsible for man's life being nasty, brutish and short in the state of nature, and his conclusion that an absolute sovereign is the only remedy to ensure a rancour-free society and prevent men from manifesting the ugly side of their nature, were efforts to create an enduring civil environment for the individual. Moreover, to assuage any doubts about Hobbes's conception of the state of nature as a condition of lawlessness, with no authority, no government, no security, no justice, total liberty and force as the only arbiter in deciding issues, all one has to do is to examine the state of men during a civil war.

Let's share power: Locke's *Two Treatises of Government* John Locke's political thoughts are set out in his *Two Treatises of Government*. Like Hobbes, Locke started his political theorizing with a treatment of the state of nature. In this state, there is perfect freedom and equality. Every man is both judge and executioner of the law of nature. And men, being partial to themselves, are likely to judge in their favour; and ill-nature, passion and revenge will probably carry them too far in punishing others. Given that men possess reason, however, they will realize that they need common consent for their general good. It is to preserve their property – their life, liberty and estate – that men quit their executive power of the law of nature and agree to have a set of written laws and an independent judge to decide disputes. The emergence of civil society is thus an outcome of a common consent to invest the legislature with political power.

For Locke, absolute monarchy is inconsistent with civil society, and so can be no form of civil government at all. Instead of being the panacea that one perceives in Hobbes, an absolute monarchy in Locke's account is more like returning men to the state of nature, since a king alone has both legislative and executive power; he is also the judge. Locke believes that decentralization of power is a prerequisite of a civil society. Instead of absolute monarchy there should be a division of powers, to ensure a separation between those who administer the laws and those who make them. This is to prevent any one arm of government from making or executing the law in its own private interest. Given this, no arm of government is above the law and the people retain the right to withdraw their allegiance from a government that is not working in their interests.

Locke made it clear that the state came into existence as a practical necessity and the main purpose of government is to protect the property of the people. According to him, 'the great and chief end, therefore, of men's uniting into commonwealths, and putting themselves under government, is the preservation of their property; to which in the state of nature there are many things wanting'.[4] By giving up all their natural power to the society which they enter into, men came to be governed by declared laws made by those into whose hands the community has put legislative power.

To ensure that those in power do not overstep their bounds, Locke delimited this legislative power. There should be a uniform law for the people. Locke is emphatic on the need for ruling power to govern by declared and received laws as against extemporary dictats and undetermined resolutions, as this is likely to return man to a condition far worse than the state of nature. In addition, the laws designed for the people should have no other end in view but their common good. Again, although there is need for government to be maintained through taxes, Locke leaves the power of such levy with the people. He asserts (quoted in Ayer 1946: 199) that 'the supreme power cannot take from any man any part of his property without his own consent'. And finally, since legislative power is delegated from the people, it cannot be transferred. The people are obliged to obey only those laws made by those authorized to legislate.

Locke's overemphasis on the protection of property as the distinctive purpose of the state has been criticized as betraying his low, materialistic view of persons. But there is a greater charge. The point of the 'contract' presupposes that it is only property owners who can give their consent, since they are the ones who have so much to lose if the state of nature persists. As such, they are the ones qualified to appoint the government by virtue of their full citizenship. To contain this curious double standard, Locke identifies two types of consent: the explicit and the tacit. If an unpropertied man enjoys the rights and privileges of a citizen of a state, then he is assumed to have given his consent tacitly. This way, he should abide by the laws of that state. The fact that the law may not be in his interest and that he is not in a position to dismiss the authority is not important to Locke.

The above shortcomings notwithstanding, Locke's influence and the importance of his political thought are immense. But perhaps his merit is nowhere as sharply articulated as in Thomas Jefferson's (1963: 153) declaration of independence:

> we hold these truths to be self-evident; that all men are created equal; that they are endowed by their creator with certain inalienable Rights; that among these are Life, Liberty, and the pursuit of Happiness. That, to secure these Rights, Governments are instituted among men, deriving their just powers from the consent of the governed – That, whenever any form of Government becomes destructive of these ends, it is the Right of the People to alter or abolish it, and to institute new Government, laying its foundation on such principles, and organizing its powers in such form, as to them shall seem most likely to effect their safety and Happiness.

Equally, the relevance of Locke's position, that powers of government should be decentralized and that the essence of government is to protect the common good, has not lessened in the more than three centuries that separate Locke's writing from our time. Ryan (1998: 385) observes: 'Locke's concern to keep government within limits by insisting that its business was with the goods of this earthly life and not with the salvation of its subjects' souls is one we find congenial.' There is to be found at least a strand of Locke's ideas of natural rights in the constitution of most countries – Nigeria, the United States and France, among many others.

Material condition determines all: Marx's 'Manifesto of the Communist Party' Marx argues that economic factors play a deciding role in creating a society that will cater for man's best interests. In the 'Manifesto of the Communist Party', Marx and Engels (1968: 51) posed the question: 'Does it require deep intuition to comprehend that man's ideas, views and conceptions, in one word, man's consciousness, changes with every change in the conditions of his material existence, in his social relations and in his social life?'

The material base is the basic factor determining man's response to his existence – moral, intellectual, artistic and, of course, political. For this reason, a capitalist society, because of the kind of relationship that exists between the owners of production and labour, cannot serve man's political ends. In a capitalist society, workers are alienated from the products of their labour, themselves, and even their fellow workers. Marx believes that this unsatisfactory condition can be set right by the proletariat coming to an awareness of its power and then overthrowing the oppressor and recovering all that has been expropriated from it.

This overthrow will not come easily, since both the proletariat and the bourgeoisie will be unwilling to give up their positions. At this point, social action, a revolution in whatever form – willingness to use violence, bloodshed, war, force – is needed to resolve the conflict. This will lead to the collapse of capitalism and the institution of socialism. This proletariat's ascension is, however, a transitional stage. The ideal society is a communist one, a 'classless' society. The state will be banished and with it the avenue for promoting the interests of a particular class. It is only at this stage that mankind will start to enjoy the freedom a political society should provide.

There are many criticisms one could make of Marx's political philosophy. His belief that communism is the 'best' and 'end' state in man's political development and historically inevitable, based on the dialectical forces of conflict that are part of human history, neglects the fact that communism may at some point also show the same kind of internal stresses that have characterized all preceding historical ages. Even taking for granted that labour will overthrow capital because of its numerical strength, Marx fails to recognize that wars are often not won by sheer strength of numbers but by scientific advancement. Britain effectively colonized many nations based on its scientific advancement. In addition, even in the so-called 'classless' societies some people will still have to provide some kind of direction. The issue of dictatorship cannot be completely ruled out, given man's nature.

In spite of these criticisms (or perhaps because of them), it is easy to perceive the influence of Marx's political philosophy on some major nations of the world (the old Soviet Union and China) and on individuals (Stalin, Mao, Castro) who have defined the fate of huge numbers of people. Even in this twenty-first century, the influence of Marx's thought is still evident in the worldwide outrage against the ills of capitalism. The anti-capitalist protesters who attempted to disrupt the G8 summit in Genoa, Italy in July 2001 provide one such indication of people's feeling concerning capitalism. The placards' carried by the demonstrators read 'zero debt' and 'people not profits'. It is difficult to disassociate such slogans from Marx's political thoughts.

Marx appears to have succeeded in shifting thinkers' focus from philosophical attempts at understanding the world to a sociological interest in changing it through a revolution in which the exploited class will overthrow their exploiters. The two legacies that Marx would not want to compromise are these: that it is the material base that determines the level of political awareness; and that a revolution carried out in order to bring about social justice is justified.

Passive resistance is the answer: Gandhi's 'Means and Ends'
Mohandas K. Gandhi tries to redirect man to his spiritual essence with its impulses towards equity, justice, freedom and non-violence. Where Marx sees a natural antagonism between capital and labour, Gandhi sees interdependence, and focuses on how both can be useful for the collective good. Equally, Gandhi does not share Marx's understanding that revolution is a necessary step in bringing about a desired political change. For him, non-violent protest, passive resistance, is the answer. He believes that there is an intimate connection between means and ends and insists that the maxim 'as is the God, so is the votary' is worth considering (Gandhi 2000: 621).

Gandhi's mission was to free Indians from colonial rule, which he insisted could be achieved without 'a drop of blood'. Non-co-operation is logical and harmless because 'it is the inherent right of a subject to refuse to assist a government that will not listen to him' (ibid.: 625). Besides, Gandhi believes that 'no government can subsist if the people cease to serve it' (ibid.).

Of course, Gandhi recognizes that suffering is indispensable to the attainment of freedom. His method is to liberate the individual, restore self-respect through self-discipline and -denial. To emphasize his message, Gandhi engaged in a plethora of disciplined activities, ranging from sweeping up others' excrement to reviving Indian handicrafts. He renounced his comfortable life to join the masses. Through his handicraft (symbolized by the spinning wheel) he effected a physical bond between the masses and the elite by inspiring both to wear khadi cloth. Gandhi decried the impact of technology on human life and advocated a technology-free society. He wanted people to realize the adverse effect technology will ultimately have on mankind's spiritual growth, and even the economy. Nelson Mandela (1999: 93) puts this succinctly: 'as we find ourselves in jobless economies, societies in which small minorities consume while the masses starve, we find ourselves forced to rethink the rationale of our current globalization and to ponder the Gandhian alternative'.

Gandhi's political vision of a simple society can seem overly romantic, even a bit backward. It is unlikely that his philosophy of non-violence would have helped the Jews in combating Hitler's unprecedented savagery. It is equally a matter of speculation whether Indian liberty was won by the long years of passive resistance and its moral strength, or by the violence that attended Gandhi's Quit India call in 1942. His pacifist stance was also powerless to stop Muslims and Hindus killing each other, especially after the partition that created the new Muslim state of Pakistan in 1947. His violent death at the hands of a Hindu fanatic also provides a tragically ironic counterweight to his political position.

And yet the way a person lives his or her life can be evaluated by looking at their enduring impact on people's lives. Although Socrates and Jesus Christ were prematurely killed, the visions they left behind have not dimmed in the two millennia that separate their time from ours. It is a mark of Gandhi's enduring influence that he is frequently mentioned alongside these great personages, in a list which is relatively short.

There is also no doubt that Gandhi's concept of non-violent resistance did help to liberate India. This is evident in the Viceroy's negotiation with him regarding Indian Independence, even though Gandhi held no elective office and represented no government. As for his legacy, it is almost impossible to think of individual freedom, social justice, political liberty, religious tolerance and, of course, passive resistance and non-violent protest without acknowledging Gandhi as the quintessential thinker in this area.

His political thought also inspired other political thinkers in their search for social change. Martin Luther King, Jr, and Nelson Mandela are good examples. Mandela credits Gandhi with shaping the liberation movements in both India and South Africa. According to him, the 'Gandhian influence dominated freedom struggles on the African continent right up to the 1960s because of the power it generated and the unity it forged among the apparently powerless. Nonviolence was the official stance of all major African coalitions, and the South African A.N.C. remained implacably opposed to violence for most of its existence' (ibid.: 92). Again, it is a tribute to Gandhi that it is the military leaders of India and Pakistan who are called upon to take the critical first step towards a non-violent twenty-first-century moral transformation of the world. The reason is simple: their Gandhian background has equipped them with the spiritual and non-violent resources and courage needed for their task (Paige 2000). Gandhi's philosophy of non-violence is at the heart of hopes for a better alternative in this current century (ibid.; Galtung 2000).

Whatever reservations we may have about Gandhi's political thought, they would not be that it cannot be put into practice – even though such practice may prove difficult for a mere mortal. Certainly, Gandhi was aware that his philosophy is not easily followed. He admits that 'it takes a fairly strenuous course of training to attain to a mental state of nonviolence' (Gandhi 2000: 626). The point is that Gandhi, more than all the philosophers already discussed, bridged the gap between political theorizing and practice. Action was his domain; he *became* the change that he sought, and 'he shines as a conscience for the world' (McGeary 1999: 91).

The above summaries of the preoccupations of political philosophers can be used as a guide in determining whether Achebe and Ngugi qualify as political thinkers. Whether we consider Plato's philosopher-king or Hobbes's absolute sovereign or Marx's classless society, their concerns are the same. They wanted to guarantee a just and fair society. The issues they reflected on included: how should political concepts such as power, authority, alienation, leadership, citizenship, ideology (among others) be understood? What is the best type of government for human society? What political institutions and social practices should be adopted to achieve the good life? What should be the value of human life? How should political institutions be arranged? What should be the nature of the authority the state exercises over its subjects? Should authority be constitutionally limited or absolute? Does the individual have a moral obligation to obey the laws of the state? What should be the nature of the individual's obligation to the state? Are there circumstances under which politically inspired disobedience is justifiable? What should be the nature of the relationship between states? Are there any circumstances under which a state can justifiably claim authority over another? How should individuals in a state relate to each other? In short, what are the basic rules that should guide mankind's collective life? To quote David Miller (1998: 500),

> Political philosophers seek to establish basic principles that will, for instance, justify a particular form of state, show that individuals have certain inalienable rights, or tell us how a society's material resources should be shared among its members. This usually involves analysing and interpreting ideas like freedom, justice, authority and democracy and then applying them in a critical way to the social and political institutions that currently exist.

These problems, however, have not yielded to any final solution. The political questions that have engaged philosophers for more than two millennia are still very much with us. In continuing the search, there is a need to evolve new languages and new techniques. It is in this light that the creative writers Achebe and Ngugi are examined.

Achebe and Ngugi as political thinkers

Achebe: political arrangements Achebe sees his writing career predominantly as a political mission: to challenge the mischievous, dangerous and unfounded view of Africa by the West as 'the heart of darkness' peopled by savages, lacking in intelligible socio-political systems. As far as he is concerned, he would be quite satisfied if his novels (especially the ones he set in the past) did no more than teach his readers that 'their past – with all its imperfections – was not one long night of savagery from which the first European acting on God's behalf delivered them'.[5]

See things for yourself: *Things Fall Apart* *Things Fall Apart* (TFA) (Achebe 1958) marks the beginning of this project. In contrast to the Western portrayal of Africa as 'the other world', 'a place of negations' peopled by savages, TFA presents a people with a clearly defined culture and an articulate political system. Simon Gikandi (1991: 202) groups TFA among works that 'tried to rehabilitate the identity and history of the African character, to assert the validity of African cultures, and to expose the violence which colonial domination had brought to bear on African societies'.

TFA portrays the political climate in Umuofia and other neighbouring villages. Solid achievements are shown as resting on qualities such as strength, hard work, perseverance, courage, determination and suchlike. Okonkwo's rise from poverty, for instance, embodies all these qualities and exposes the superficiality of the charge of laziness often levelled against the African, which the colonizer uses to justify ill-treatment.

Although Okonkwo is a great wrestler, society is structured in such a way that he cannot use his strength to molest others or take what does not belong to him by force. He is fined for beating his wife, denigrated for his brusque attitude to Osugo, and has to borrow yams from Nwakibie to start his farm. The only times he intentionally kills are during wars and in obedience to the mandate of the oracle: the killing of Ikemefuna. Even after this, he is filled with remorse and unable to eat for three days because of the special relationship that had existed between him and the boy he has killed. On the one occasion he inadvertently kills a kinsman, he is exiled for seven years.

All this is possible because of the political system in Umuofia, in which the *ndichie* (council of elders) rules collectively, taking decisions on behalf of the clan. The council's main interest is to ensure a harmonious, thriving and respected community for the people. For instance the decision to send an emissary to Mbaino is taken only after many people have spoken in favour of the motion. Any problem that cannot be handled by the council of elders is referred to the *egwugwu*, the cult of the masked spirit, the highest judicial body in traditional Igbo society, made up of nine members, each representing a village of the clan, and headed by Ajofia.

The cases brought before the *egwugwu* are judged in the full assembly of the people. Each party to the dispute is allowed to present his or her case, as exemplified in the dispute between Uzowulu and his in-laws. Witnesses are called, after which the *egwugwu* retires to its 'underground home' to deliberate. It is the responsibility of Ajofia to declare the verdict. Thus he acts as a judge and the other cult members as the jury. It must be noted that the principal interest of the *egwugwu* is to ensure that justice is done in the settlement, rather than to apportion blame or praise.

This high political order ensures that crimes are kept at a minimum. For instance, when Okonkwo breaks the week of peace it is 'the first time for many years'; 'even the oldest men could only remember one or two other occasions somewhere in the dim past' (p. 22).

The political cohesion in Umuofia also spreads to neighbouring villages. Although the people of Mbanta admit that they have no king, they 'have men of high title and the chief priests and the elders' (p. 105). These leaders are qualified to take decisions and act on behalf of the people, as exemplified in their decision to give a portion of the evil forest to the missionaries. Robert Wren (1981: 18) notes that to the colonials 'the stateless society of the Igbo was anarchistic. They were unaware of a democratic balance that *ozo* achieved and maintained.' Noteworthy is the fact that the credentials that qualify these people to form the governing council of Mbanta are specified, just as we know what qualified Okonkwo to become one of the 'lords' in Umuofia. Contrary to the Western conception of Africa as the 'antithesis of civilization', *TFA* indicates that Africa has a sound political past.

All this changes with the coming of the white man to Africa. The democratic structure of Umuofia, with its widespread political power, is forcibly replaced by the administration of a district commissioner, who has to rely on interpreters drawn from the dregs of society – 'the excrement of the clan' (p. 101) – after giving them a modicum of education. So a system that had previously known direct governance comes under governance through interpretation.

The result is a complete upheaval. The white man's prison becomes 'full of men who had offended against the white man's law' (p. 123). Respect for elders and tradition are thrown overboard as the incidents of the treatment the court messengers and interpreters mete out to the six Umuofia leaders and Enoch's unmasking of the *egwugwu*, respectively, signify. Moreover, bribery becomes institutionalized as part of government policy – Nnama's family win the land dispute simply by bribing the court messengers and interpreters. Leadership through lies and reckless use of power becomes a way of life. The DC's invitation to the leaders of Umuofia for a peace mission concerning Enoch ends by jailing the men without even hearing their side of the story and imposing a fine of two hundred bags of cowries on them. Typically, the court messengers collect a fine of two hundred and fifty bags of cowries from the people.

It is instructive that the event that precipitates the major crisis between the Umuofia community and the white administration is caused by one of the converts, Enoch. As an associate of the white man's administration, Enoch has no qualms about committing the highest crime in the land: unmasking an *egwugwu*, the symbol of his society's hidden secret and power. (Charles Nnolim [1992: 26] rightly interprets the 'unmasking of the *egwugwu* as the unmasking of the clan'.) And, as might be expected, it is the leaders of Umuofia who rise in defence of their age-old tradition, only to be imprisoned, humiliated and fined.

When in the end Okonkwo, that passionate defender of his tradition, commits his first intentional murder, beheading the head messenger, it becomes difficult to classify it as an act of savagery. Pius Dada (1986: 30) points out that 'Okonkwo stands as a monumental epic character who maintains his stand against the powers and customs of Europeans'. Ngugi (1972: 28) believes that 'violence in order to change an intolerable, unjust social order is not savagery: it purifies man'. For him, characters such as Okonkwo, with their every gesture in their interaction with nature and with their social environment, are a vivid reminder of the fact that 'Africa was not a land of perpetual childhood passed over by history as it passed from East to West to find its highest expression in the Western empires of the twentieth century' (Ngugi 1993: 3–4). Okonkwo's subsequent suicide, then, is possibly a statement of his complete belief in his own political system and his utter rejection of the white man's system.

Nothing stands alone: *Arrow of God* In *Arrow of God* (AOG) (Achebe 1964) the story is similar. Winterbottom, in an attempt to effect the colonial system of indirect rule, decides to make Ezeulu – the symbol of the religious and political unity of the six villages that make up Umuaro – a warrant chief. He is completely unprepared for Ezeulu declining his invitation, and interprets it as an insult. The fact that Ezeulu already has political powers that cannot be readily *surrendered* is not considered, because such power is seen as unimportant. Instead, he demands that Ezeulu be arrested, and his consequent imprisonment for two months prevents him from performing a religious rite (announcing the appearance of a new moon and eating a sacred yam) which also acts as a political bond for the people. This is the major factor that triggers the reactions that completely destabilize the political set-up in Umuaro.

Reflections on *Things Fall Apart* and *Arrow of God* These two novels invite reflection on many counts. There is the issue of law and justice. The treatment meted out to the leaders of Umuofia and Ezeulu for daring to uphold the tradition of their land calls the reader's attention to the notion of law and justice. Should the law of one country be imposed on another when it does not represent that community's opinion of acceptable behaviour, as demonstrated by the incidents that lead to the imprisonment of the six leaders of Umuofia and Ezeulu? Should law serve an oligarchical interest? Should justice not embody the idea of equity and impartiality? Should a law that does not promote justice and common good be obeyed? What is the place of interpretation in the dispensation of justice? Is it justified for a people to obey laws they do not understand? Does any nation have the right to impose its laws on another, especially without taking cognisance of the already existing laws? In the case of resistance, whose right should be respected? What should be the nature of the political relationship that exists between a powerful nation and a less powerful one? What is the justification for considering a people's political system unsuitable for them? How should an individual react to political oppression? What is power and how can it be exercised responsibly? Should those who execute or administer the laws also make them?

There is also the issue of the legitimacy of political power. Should the will of the people legitimize power? Or should it be imposed on people without any regard to their consent? AOG clearly reveals the source of Ezeulu's power, 'from behind the heavy tread of all the people gave me strength' (p. 71). On the other hand, Winterbottom's assertion that he won't have 'his' natives thinking they can treat the administration with contempt (p. 49) leaves the reader wondering how 'the natives' come to be Winterbottom's property.

Also important is the idea of political revolution and under what condition(s) it is justified. In TFA, the egwugwu embarks on the destruction of the white man's 'shrine' to cleanse the land of the sacrilege Enoch committed by unmasking an egwugwu and also to put an end to the white man's religion, which is destroying the people's way of life. Revolution becomes a corrective political measure, especially when it is enacted with the consent of the people. The decision to wage war against the white man is taken by the clansmen.

Okonkwo's action in beheading the head messenger to the white man is a call to his people to resist political oppression. That his action fails to get the support of his clansmen raises further issues. Can an individual act for his society without the people's mandate? What are the limits of an individual's right in a society? Achebe seems to suggest that an individual's right to act for his society should be guided by a majority decision. D. D. Raphael (1976: 11) shares this opinion: if each individual is allowed to act on the basis of what he or she thinks is right, then the system becomes unworkable. Equally, in AOG, Ezeulu's refusal to listen to the voice of the people as represented by the ten men of high title that came to him to resolve the New Yam Feast problem results in the people's defection and his loss of relevance. To them Ezeulu's fall is simple; 'no man however great was greater than his people; that no one ever won judgment against his clan' (p. 230).

Ngugi: political arrangements Ngugi, through his novels, also insists that Africans have their own system of values, steeped in long, tested and evolving traditions, which are seriously disturbed by colonial intervention. According to him (Ngugi 1972: 41), the African 'colonial middle class education and brainwashing told him that he had no history. The black man did not really exist, had slept in the dark continent until the Livingstones and the Stanleys woke him into history.' He sees the task of the African writer as that of restoring the African character to his history, and resuming the broken dialogue with the gods of his people (ibid.: 43).

See the rift you caused: *The River Between* *The River Between* (*TRB*) (Ngugi 1965) describes the gradual penetration of the white man into African society and the political crisis that results. Using religion as a political instrument, the white man is able to widen the rivalry between the people of Makuyu and Kameno ridges of Kenya. The disintegration of Joshua's family serves to mirror this crisis in the community.

Joshua, a Christian convert from Makuyu, disowns his only two children, Muthoni (for yearning for a link with the tradition of her people and allowing herself to be circumcised), and Nyambura (for falling in love with Waiyaki, a non-Christian, from Kameno).

The Kameno people see themselves as the protectors of the purity of the tribe. They form the *kiama* to give political expression to the need to uphold their tribal independence. Waiyaki's action in associating with a Christian is interpreted by the *kiama* as an act of betrayal. His vision of uniting the people, Christians and non-Christians, into a strong political force is scuttled by both sides. He is condemned to death by the *kiama* in spite of the tremendous contributions he made to society and despite his vision of leading the people 'into a political movement that would shake the whole country, that would tell the white man "Go!"' (p. 151).

Waiyaki's death acts as a symbol of the waste of human resources visited on the African community as a result of colonial intervention. This point is also aptly made in *TFA*, when Obierika, looking at the dangling body of Okonkwo, turns to the District Commissioner and says, 'that man was one of the greatest men in Umuofia. You drove him to kill himself ... ' (p. 147).

This is our land: *Weep Not, Child* *Weep Not, Child* (*WNC*) (Ngugi 1964) also reveals some of the factors responsible for the political crisis in African communities. The Kenyans forced to fight in the First

World War, as represented by Ngotho, come back to discover that their land is gone. This forces Ngotho to become a squatter and to work for a white man, Mr Howland, on the land that rightly should have been his own – a land that once belonged to his ancestors. This situation worsens with the Second World War. Boro, Ngotho's son, back from the Second World War, discovers that he has lost his roots in the tribe – there is no land to settle on and no employment from the government he has gone to war for. His bitterness leads him to join the Mau Mau freedom fighters.

Reflections on *The River Between* and *Weep Not, Child* The reader is invited to evaluate Boro's action, and indeed, the entire Mau Mau project on the basis of the idea of law and justice that permits the 'unlawful' and 'unjust' taking of people's land and the establishment of a political power that does not enjoy the people's consent. In *TRB*, Waiyaki's political vision is sharpened by his realization of 'the shame of a people's land being taken away, the shame of being forced to work on those same lands, the humiliation of paying taxes for a government that you knew nothing about!' (p. 142). Under the colonial dispensation, with its repressive laws and total disregard for common good and people's consent, are there any grounds for political obligation? Are people not justified to revolt in the case of a government that forsakes its responsibility of catering for their well-being? Olusegun Oladipo (2001: 21–2) notes that: 'It has been suggested that the obligation which the people have to obey the directives of those who rule does not derive simply from the fact they are authorized to rule, but also from the fact that they rule in a particular manner, deviation from which is a good ground for the people's abdication of the obligation to obey.'

In WNC, the Mau Mau freedom fighters begin as the political resistance to combat the terror of government brutality against them, the repressive Emergency law, the general oppressive political atmosphere under which the blacks live, and more importantly, to reclaim the people's lands from the white man. Boro's decision to join the Mau Mau is a result of the realization of the importance of black people coming together to stop the white man's oppression. In *A Grain of Wheat* (AGOW) (Ngugi 1967) both Kihika and General R see the Mau Mau freedom fight as the only political response left to the African in an attempt to redress the political ills introduced into the African system by the white man and his black agents. *WNC* and *AGOW* present organized group action as a politically justified means of changing a system.

Political concepts

Achebe and Ngugi through their works also explore many political concepts; the major ones are alienation, power, gender, ideology, leadership and citizenship.

Alienation Alienation refers to a state of being separated from one's environment. Simply put, to be alienated is to feel detached, to be uninvolved. This is experienced when a person (or group of persons) disconnects with anything that previously meant something to them. Alienation consists in a state of feeling of estrangement from a whole, whether family, friends, neighbourhood, community, institution, workplace, Church, state, belief and so on. This feeling can come about if another person (or group of persons, government policies, social institutions and so on) disappoints expectations. Once the familiar understanding is gone, a sense of isolation and detachment is experienced. This withdrawal distances the person involved and imposes a sense of alienation on him or her.

In Achebe's *No Longer at Ease (NLAE)* (1960), Obi personifies the political disintegration in African communities caused by the white man's intervention disconnecting the African from society.

Back from England, where he had gone to further his studies, Obi is looked upon as the people's future leader. At first he watches with dismay the level of corruption in his society and is determined not to jump on the bandwagon. He sees the political hope of his society as lying in the hands of people like himself. And yet, before long, Obi succumbs to the tension imposed by the conflicting demands of his society. How does one acquire all the paraphernalia of the new system and yet still retain the ideals of one's traditional society? How does an individual change a system founded on a new order that did not take into consideration the existing political set-up? How does one change a system he or she is not an integral part of, or probably does not even understand? What is at the root of this political disconnection?

Obi's struggles provide a clue. He loses out in attempting to reconcile his Christian upbringing, his Western education and his society's vehement opposition to his proposed marriage to Clara, who is an *osu* (outcast). In traditional Igbo society it is taboo for a free-born such as Obi even to contemplate such a union. His father, who is a staunch Christian, recognizes that being a Christian is 'no reason to marry an *osu*' (p. 120), because '*osu* is like leprosy in the minds of our people' (p. 121). Obi also finds it difficult to achieve a balance between his society's expectation of his living standard as a member of an elite and the demands made on him by his position. In the end he slides into corruption.

Obi's political rootlessness is further demonstrated by his inability to be a part of the government for which he works. He sees this government as something apart from him. Although he is not worried about local leave being abolished, he feels that it is 'for government to decide' (p. 139). Mr Green's response that 'it's people like you who ought to make the government decide. That is what I have always said. There is no single Nigerian who is prepared to forgo a little privilege in the interests of his country ... And you tell me you want to govern yourselves' (p. 139) although probably spoken in malice, nevertheless has a ring of truth. Obi's attitude fails to match his analysis that what is needed to turn the country round are fresh graduates. The fact that Obi can only theorize about this, but is unable to act when the need arises, shows his understanding of his involvement in government affairs.

Unfortunately Obi's alienation is a reflection of the general attitude. 'In Nigeria the government was "they". It had nothing to do with you or me. It was an alien institution and people's business was to get as much from it as they could without getting into trouble' (pp. 29–30). This is evident in people's expectations of their leaders. Where Ezeani in *TFA* rejects Okonkwo's *kola* because he broke the week of peace (p. 21), Joseph's colleague takes it for granted that because Obi is the secretary to the Scholarship Board, 'E go make plenty money there. Every student who wan go England go de see am for house' (p. 70). And this turns out to be correct, as the cases of Miss Mark and others reveal. The only question the sole representative of one of the three regions of Nigeria who slept all through Obi's interview wakes up to ask him is 'Why do you want a job in the civil service? So that you can take bribes?' (p. 36). Although Obi treats this question with disdain, it ends up as his undoing. Even a minister of state is known to have said that the trouble is not in receiving bribes, but in failing to do the thing for which the bribe is given (p. 80). It is, therefore, no surprise that Obi's fall is not seen as something bad in itself but rather as his inability to apply the rules of the game: 'Obi tried to do what everyone does without finding out how it was done' (p. 5).

Has it ever been thus? Achebe seems to suggest in *TFA* that bribery became a way of life with the coming of the white man. The white man's messengers and interpreters exploit the barrier in communication caused by language and the fear the white man's power invokes in the natives. For instance, Nnama's family win a land dispute by bribing the messengers and interpreters (p. 124). When the District

Commissioner fined the leaders of Umuofia two hundred bags of cowries, his court messengers collect fifty extra bags from the people (pp. 137–9). In *AOG*, Chief Ikedi teams up with the road overseer to extort money from the people under the guise that the order was from 'the white man' (p. 37).

When Mr Green explains Obi's accepting bribes: 'the African is corrupt through and through' (p. 3), one wonders what type of analysis justifies such a conclusion. Is the assessment based on the understanding of the African in the pre-colonial environment? Or is it grounded in the socio-political forces in place that invariably shape a character such as Obi? In *TFA*, an eminent man such as Obi's grandfather, Okonkwo, who has set his mind on taking the highest titles in the clan, is banished from Umuofia for seven years for a crime he committed inadvertently. There is no room for him to use bribes to mitigate his punishment.

The point is not that the white man came intentionally to set up a government founded on giving and receiving bribes. His system of administration, however (indirect rule exacerbated by the language barrier), coupled with total disregard of the existing political system, provided an environment conducive to bribery, and it became institutionalized, part of government procedure. When at the end 'everybody wondered why' Obi took a bribe, it becomes apparent that their reflection is limited to the present – Obi is an epitome of the modern African, an educated young man with a bright future.

But in thus symbolizing the modern African, Obi also becomes the product of the white man's political suppression, with its inherent pressure on African political systems. This makes it possible for Obi to become so alienated from his society that he emerges as a 'beast of no nation' (p. 138) in a society where his grandfather was once one of the 'lords' of the land.

NLAE does not, however, consider Obi blameless. His lack of commitment to building up his society as the 'son of the soil' is portrayed as offensive. Instead of using his education to reintegrate himself into his society, Obi uses it as a screen to fence off that society. He entangles himself in the struggle for personal liberation at the point he should have been leading his people in the struggle for political liberation. His failure guides the reader into an assessment of the true place of the individual in society. To what extent can an individual's conduct determine the political progress of, or effect a change in, society? And what method will guarantee the most or least success?

In *WNC*, Ngugi portrays alienation in the way Africans are dispossessed of their land. Even when Boro decides to join the Mau Mau in order to fight for the reclamation of the land, he discovers that he has been so alienated that he is not fighting for the cause of his society but simply 'to kill and rejoice at any who falls under my sword' (p. 116). Kamau's remarks perhaps best sum up the general feeling of alienation: 'There's no safety anywhere. There's no hiding in this naked land' (p. 94). By showing the effects alienation has on their characters, Achebe and Ngugi help expose the conditions that can bring about political crisis and the social evils that can destabilize government.

Power Power in politics can take many forms. Typically, it is the ability of one person to exercise authority, strong influence or even absolute rule on another, to the point of getting total compliance by any means possible. Achebe and Ngugi portray the adverse consequences of focusing on politics solely as the use of power at the expense of utilizing it for the expression of responsible public choice.

Achebe's *TFA* shows how the African traditional system, with its in-built checks and balances, is supplanted by the white man's administration by force. Where the traditional system of Umuofia had ready measures to control cases of power abuse (such as punishing Okonkwo for beating his wife during the week of peace), the white man's administration made it possible for power to be used recklessly, not just by the white man, but also by his black associates in his name. The treatment given to the six leaders of Umuofia by the District Commissioner in *TFA* (p. 137) and the handling of Ezeulu's rejection of his invitation by Winterbottom in *AOG* (p. 149) are good examples of this.

As regards the associates, the attitude of the messengers and interpreters to the six leaders of Umuofia in *TFA* (p. 138) is an instructive example. Also, Enoch does not hesitate to unmask an *egwugwu* – the symbol of his society's hidden secret and power – because to him the white man's power is unassailable (p. 131).

In *AOG* the situation is no different. Working under the white man's administration, Chief James Ikedi, a warrant chief, sees power as something that can be manipulated for personal benefit. He teams up with the road overseer to extort money from his people. Although Captain Winterbottom does not know it, it is, nevertheless, the white man's system that provides an environment suitable for such misuse of power. Merely telling his people that 'the overseer was carrying out the orders of the white man' (p. 57) is enough to guarantee instant obedience, despite the fact that this is a people used to questioning the wisdom of their leaders and (occasionally) that of their gods. Nwaka not only challenges the authenticity of Ezeulu's account as regards the land dispute between them and the people of Okperi, but ends by getting the support of the people (pp. 16–17). In *TFA*, Nwakibie tells the story of Obiako, who went to consult the oracle and was told that his dead father wanted a goat for a sacrifice. In reply Obiako tells the oracle to ask his dead father if he ever had a fowl when he was alive (p. 15). What, then, is responsible for this kind of ready compliance on the part of a people used to challenging authority? Is it born out of coercive force or prudential obligation? *TFA* provides a useful insight through the account of how the white man wiped out the Abame people (p. 98) and the kind of fear this created in other neighbouring villages. Power in this instance is exercised as coercion.

Such misuse of power is also evident in the attitude of the court messenger sent to Umuaro by Winterbottom to bring Ezeulu. He asserts his superiority by telling his audience 'how kaputin Winta-bortom has put me in charge of many of his affairs' (p. 138). He goes on to tell Ezeulu, 'If you do me well I shall arrange for you to see him tomorrow. Everything is in my hands; if I say that the white man will see this person, he will see him' (p. 139). In addition, although Ezeulu had set out on his own to answer the white man's call before the policemen sent to arrest him arrived at his house, the corporal still tells the people in Ezeulu's house that 'we cannot come and go for nothing. When a masked spirit visits you you have to appease it footprints with presents. The white man is the masked spirit of today' (p. 154). Akuebue's reply, 'very true ... the masked spirit of our day is the white man and his messengers', perhaps best sums up the power politics introduced to Africa by the white man. Without a mask he is able to inspire terror and fright in the minds of the people, just as their masked spirit does. By exercising power as the 'construction of incentives' the people are left with no other acceptable option but to obey. According to W. Phillips Shively (1997: 6), power may be exercised as such a construction when 'we make the alternative so unattractive that only one reasonable option remains'.

The unbridled use of power is also a dominant theme in *A Man of the People* (*AMOP*) (Achebe 1966). With independence, the leaders see their new status as an effective political weapon in the silencing of any form of opposition. The Minister of Finance, a first-rate economist, is disgraced and ejected from his office for drawing up a plan to deal with the slump in the international coffee market which the Prime Minister fears will not augur well for his political consolidation. So instead of 'risk[ing] losing the election by cutting down the price paid to coffee planters at that critical moment' (p. 3), he instructs the

National Bank to print fifteen million pounds, dismisses the Minister of Finance and his supporters and proceeds to broadcast to the nation that the 'dismissed Ministers were conspirators and traitors who had teamed up with foreign saboteurs to destroy the new nation'. As a result the Minister of Finance's car is destroyed by angry mobs and his house stoned. Another dismissed minister is pulled out of his car, 'beaten insensible, and dragged along the road for fifty yards, then tied hand and foot, gagged and left by the roadside' (p. 5).

When Chief Nanga's attempt to bribe Odili to step down for him at the next parliamentary election fails, he arranges for Odili to lose his job. Odili's father is removed as the chairman of P.O.P. in Urua for allowing Odili's party to launch their campaign in his house (p. 132). Further, his tax is reassessed not based on his known pension of eighty-four pounds a year, 'but on an alleged income of five hundred pounds derived from "business"'. This is followed almost immediately by the visit of three local council policemen, looking like marijuana smokers, to arrest him. He is manhandled before Odili finds the money to pay. This is not all. Seven public works lorries are sent to Odili's village to 'cart away the pipes they had deposited several months earlier' (p. 133) for the community's project rural water scheme. Some of the pipes are returned two days later, after Odili's village publicly denounces him and reaffirms its support for Chief Nanga. Odili is mercilessly beaten up for attending Chief Nanga's inaugural campaign meeting and subsequently framed for being in possession of dangerous weapons, a ploy to prevent him from signing his nomination paper for the election. Max, the leader of Odili's party, is killed when he tries to investigate the charge that his political opponent Chief Koko's wife is leading the women's wing of the P.O.P. in an operation to smuggle into the polling booths wads of ballot paper concealed in their brassieres (p. 142). At the end, however, Chief Koko also loses his life. The unassailability of power is upturned to expose its fragile and illusory security.

Several questions are raised: is power used to the best advantage? That is, is power used to provide the most suitable solution to a shared problem, while allowing reasonable latitude for public choices?

Through an artistic exploration of power at both communal and individual levels, Achebe's novels create vivid awareness in the mind of the reader of the limits of power, its destructive capacity and rude consequences.

Ngugi also details the many guises power can assume to secure compliance and render alternatives impossible. In WNC, to force obedience on the people, the government declares a state of Emergency.

This provides cover to deal with blacks suspected of being anti-government. Ngotho is labelled a Mau Mau leader and his family placed under close surveillance. His wife, Njeri, and his son, Kori, are arrested in their compound for breaking the curfew law. Although there is a fixed fine for breaking the curfew, when the money is paid only Njeri is released; Kori is sent instead to a detention camp without trial (p. 92). Eventually, when Ngotho plays into government hands by confessing to a murder he did not commit, his whole family (except Boro, who is in the forest) is arrested and brutalized. By the time he is released, he can only go home and die (p. 141). The fate of Ngotho's family exemplifies the general political climate. Many people are arrested in their homes under the pretext of their having broken the curfew law; some are brutally murdered by being dubbed Mau Mau terrorists. The killing of the barber, along with five other men – 'four of them had been some of the richest people and quite influential in all the land' (p. 97) – and teacher Isaka, are a few examples.

Equally, Mr Howland, from his position as District Commissioner, regards power as a weapon of destruction. Blacks for him are mere 'savages', fit only to destroy each other. Although he despises Jacobo because he is a savage, he nevertheless sees him as a tool to be used in destroying other blacks. He makes him a chief and the leader of the home guard and invests him with a great deal of power. Jacobo, of course, utilizes this 'advantage' to the point where his name becomes 'a terror in the land'; his appearance is a cause for people to dash into the bush; his approach to someone's home is an automatic sign of danger (p. 104). This undeniably gives Mr Howland 'a certain gratifying pleasure', to see the machine he has set in motion working; 'the blacks were destroying the blacks' (p. 110).

The use of power to compel obedience also continues in *AGOW*. The people of Thabai are forced out of their old village, their huts burnt down and all African trading centres closed 'in the interests of peace and security' because of the 'fall of Mahee police post to Kihika and his band of forest fighters' (p. 123). In addition, the people of Thabai are made to pay for offering help to Kihika even after he has been caught and hanged by the government. They are forced to dig a trench that will surround the whole village. The soldiers and the home guards beat up any person who as much as raises his or her back or slows down in any way. The people are made prisoners in their own village and only women are granted two hours before sunset to look for food. This time is later reduced to one hour and then completely taken away (p. 126). Twenty-one men and women die in these harsh conditions (p. 128).

Karanja remembers how his association with the white administration as a home guard had made him feel part of 'an invisible might' and gave him a 'consciousness of power' that can 'dispose of human life by merely pulling a trigger'. And, naturally, when he shot people, 'they seemed less like human beings and more like animals' (p. 199). Even in independent Kenya the situation is no different. Power is used to create a society of 'man-eat-man'. In *Devil on the Cross* (*DOTC*) (Ngugi 1982), Wangari, a peasant woman, is arrested by the senior police superintendent and his men for bringing them to apprehend hardened thieves and robbers holding a competition to determine who is the best (pp. 196–8). The superintendent instead apologizes and begs for forgiveness from the master of ceremonies for disrupting the function. The invitation of the master of ceremonies to him to join them is eagerly accepted; he sits and starts 'talking and laughing over a glass of whisky' (p. 198).

Moreover the military and police attack the procession of workers and peasants led by Muturi, the student union leader, and the workers' leader, which had hoped to stop the competition. In the course of this attack, although many of the workers lose their lives, many are fatally injured and others arrested by the senior superintendent of police, local radio reports only the death of two soldiers and Mwireri wa Mukiraai, who takes part in the competition (pp. 213–14). Wangari, Muturi and the student leader are also charged with the offence of disturbing the public peace at the golf course 'during a meeting of some *private business men*' (p. 231).

Gender Gender refers to the social construction that arises as a result of being male or female as opposed to sex, which is a biological category. Gender is a culturally produced way of seeing and representing female and male behaviour, informed by our beliefs, attitudes and values. For instance, areas of activity such as thinking and writing, which are considered prestigious, have traditionally been regarded as men's domain. In patriarchal societies (most societies in the world) gender discrimination – manifest in unequal access to economic, political, religious and social relations to the detriment of women – is presented as part of established culture. Women in such societies are predisposed to believe in and accept marginal social status. Gender discrimination may be read as a general comment on the state of gender relations in the social world: women are confined to marginal space, men dominate the centre. Such cultural stereotyping not only gives rise to imaginative and interpretative associations about male and female, but also influences our perceptions of ourselves. Gender could play a key role in determining the rate of political development in any given culture.

Achebe sees the involvement of women in politics as closely tied to stages in society's development. In the traditional Umuofia as depicted in *TFA* Ezinma (who alone among all Okonkwo's children show signs of promise) ends up without any significant input to her society. Most probably, like Okonkwo, her society 'wish[es] she were a boy' (p. 122). In spite of all that Okonkwo does, or tries to do, for his society, nothing is heard of him until his grandson, Obi, in *NLAE*, captures the imagination of the people with his brilliance and subsequent fall from grace.

Despite the closeness between Obi and his mother and the affection between him and Clara, none of the women can exert sufficient influence on him to enable him to become the kind of leader he should be. Paradoxically, it is their exit from his life (one in death, the other via severance of links) that turns him into the kind of person the society despises.

Starting with *AMOP*, with independence, more education for women and subsequent awareness of their rights, a woman's role in effecting positive change in society's political sphere becomes pronounced. Eunice, an intelligent lawyer, is one of the founding members of C.P.C. When Chief Koko engineers the brutal murder of Max, she does not hesitate to shoot him. It is significant that the novel ends on a tribute to her action as the only redeeming conduct to emerge from the 'fat-dripping, gummy, eat-and-let-eat regime just ended' (p. 149). In an interview with Jane Wilkinson (1992: 53), Achebe advocates the need to 'find a way in which the modern woman in Africa will have a role which is not just something we refer to once in a while, but brings her talents and her special gifts to the running of affairs'.

Ngugi believes that for society to function well there is need for women to contribute. In *AGOW*, during the Emergency, Wambui 'carried secrets from the villages to the forest and back to the villages and towns' (p. 19). She is so much a part of the Mau Mau struggle that she is privy to most of its movements. During the workers' meeting in 1950 to decide whether to embark on a strike which is meant to paralyse the country and make governance difficult for the white man, it is the incitement of the women led by Wambui that decides the men. Moreover, Njeri recognizes that for her love for Kihika to be meaningful she has to join him in the forest, take up arms and fight alongside him in the Mau Mau struggle for independence.

In *DOTC*, Wangari leads the police to the competition organized by thieves and robbers. Although the police end up arresting her, she remains undaunted. Instead, her steady voice, 'so you, the police force, are the servants of one class only?' (p. 198) serves to highlight further the need for proper representation in the ordering of society. Also the task of clearing what Obi in *NLAE* refers to as the 'Augean stable' (p. 40) is left to Wariinga. Her meeting with her ex-lover provides her with the opportunity to see most of the hardened thieves and robbers who participated in the thieves' and robbers' competition. She shoots her ex-lover, who is one of the robbers, and proceeds to shoot two more for their contribution in the arrest and imprisonment of those fighting for the interest of the common people. The people who try to capture her are 'greeted by judo kicks and karate chops' (p. 254). Again it is with a woman's action, with her role in redefining the political order and struggle in creating and sustaining a healthy socio-political environment that Ngugi ends *DOTC*: 'Wariinga walked on ... But she knew with all her heart that the hardest struggles of her life's journey lay ahead ... ' (p. 254).

Ideology We live in a world of choices. To be a Christian or a Muslim, to favour capitalism or communism, to belong to one political party or another, to have friends or be a recluse, etc. Our beliefs, values, ideas, prejudices, attitudes and suchlike often guide these choices. Ideology generally refers to a science of thought dealing with beliefs, notions, theories, attitudes and the like, developed by and representative of a group. The make-up of ideology can be philosophical, political, economic, religious, moral or cultural. Social movements or policies usually reflect ideology.

Achebe's works portray a body of political ideas that should form the basis of national policy. One of these ideas is the need for organized group action aimed at reforming the system. In *TFA* the *egwugwu* is able to reduce the white man's church to 'a pile of earth and ashes' (p. 135), whereas Okonkwo's lone action in beheading the white man's messenger ends in his committing suicide when he discovers that the people are not behind him. In *AOG*, Ezeulu's individual decision 'to hit Umuaro at its most vulnerable point' (p. 201) by refusing to call the New Yam Feast in spite of the entreaty of the leaders of Umuaro leads to his downfall.

Equally, in *NLAE*, Obi's assumption that he can stand 'aloof' from the corruption in society, instead of campaigning vigorously to win people to his own way of thinking so as to tackle the problem collectively, leads to his own failure as the pressure of trying to withstand corruption alone proves too difficult. Similarly, his supposition that he can act outside established values, as demonstrated by his decision to marry Clara, an *osu*, fails because of his inability to recognize that such a tradition can be changed only by the people and not by an individual.

Closely related to the idea of organized group action is the need for unity. The old man from Mbanta in *TFA* sees the problem of contemporary African society as the inability of people 'to speak with one voice' (p. 118), which is what made it possible for the white man to penetrate and spread division among the people. Obierika also sees the 'falling apart' of the clan as caused by the fact that the 'clan can no longer act like one' (p. 124).

The idea that true leadership should involve achieving a balance between action and intellectualism is also posited. In *TFA* Okonkwo's failures are based on his inability to establish this balance (or, possibly, he does not know that the two can co-exist). In *AOG* Ezeulu's conflict seems to arise from his inability to balance these two roles. Although he knows that it is his duty to be at the vanguard of his people in encountering problems, identifying and tackling them effectively, he abdicates this function and instead turns it into a weapon of punishment. In *NLAE* Obi theorizes about the country's problem and a possible solution without seeing himself as a possible candidate to bring about the desired change. Intellectuals are prevented from acting, as the cases of the Minister of Finance's dismissal and Max's murder in *AMOP* demonstrate.

Thus the failure of leaders seems to be based on the inability to marry the two concepts. According to Plato (1941: 178–9), 'unless either philosophers become kings in their countries or those who are now called kings and rulers come to be sufficiently inspired with a genuine desire for wisdom; unless, that is to say, political power and philosophy meet together ... there can be no rest from troubles'. In the same vein, Achebe (in an interview with Jane Wilkinson) asserts that it is action and reflection working together that can save the situation but realizes that 'these are the two polarities of our reality and we must expect them sometimes even to be at loggerheads' (Wilkinson 1992: 48). The challenge of true leadership, then, should be how to reconcile and utilize these two opposites.

Ngugi also believes that some ideas should form the basis for national policy in order to ensure a healthy political environment. He sees organized group revolutionary action as the means towards African recovery. In *WNC* and *AGOW*, the Mau Mau freedom fighters put up a determined resistance to white oppression. In *DOTC* Muturi sees the route towards African recovery in 'a strong organization of the workers, and peasants of the land, together with those whose eyes and ears are now open and alert' (p. 205). For him, the land should be cleansed of the clan of parasites who reap where they have not sown; they should be replaced with the producers (p. 53).

Closely related to the above is the idea that African recovery might be possible if African societies go back to their communistic way of life. The students' leader in DOTC decries the condition of African cities which, like Nairobi, are 'large, soulless and corrupt' because their economies are tailored to those of capitalist countries such as America that glorify the principle of self-interest instead of the African notion of collective good (p. 15).

The need for unity is similarly emphasized. In TRB African internecine rivalry makes it possible for the white man to penetrate and establish his political dominance over the people. Waiyaki's advice to the people to close ranks and fight in one political movement against the invader is not heeded. In WNC the result of this disunity becomes evident in the way people are dispossessed of their lands. In DOTC, Muturi recognizes that 'many hands can lift a weight, however heavy' (p. 52).

Ngugi also endorses the union of action and intellectualism as basic components of true leadership. In TRB Waiyaki recognizes that education is needed in the fight for political freedom (p. 143), although he does not live to fulfil this vision. Also in DOTC, workers, peasants, petty traders and students unite to fight the exploiters as represented by the thieves and robbers (p. 203). Muturi also invites Wariinga and Gatuiria to use their education and join the masses in their fight to create a better society. By the end of the novel this call has yielded some results, as demonstrated by Wariinga's shooting of a number of the robbers. Perhaps more than any other character she shows how the two combinations can work.

The political ideologies contained in Achebe's and Ngugi's works can provoke a critical re-evaluation of ideas and beliefs that might have been overlooked, in an effort to understand basic social facts and institute enduring national policies for their societies.

Leadership Achebe's and Ngugi's works also reveal the importance of the role of leaders in creating and maintaining a healthy political system. Achebe believes that the lack of commitment of political office-holders/seekers to identifying the nation's problems and finding solutions to them hinders political development. In Achebe's AMOP the leaders' main (or even sole) interest is to safeguard their political ambition by any means. The Prime Minister readily plunges the country into unprecedented inflation instead of accepting professional advice on how best to deal with the country's financial crisis. He fails to realize that it is the responsibility of leaders to eliminate the flaws in the organizational structure of society as well as to provide guidance and direction. According to Achebe, as quoted by Ezenwa-Oheato (1997: 249), 'leadership is a sacred trust like the priesthood in civilized humane religions. No one gets into it lightly or inadvisedly because it demands qualities of mind and discipline of body and will [extend] far beyond the needs of the ordinary citizen.' Chief Nanga also sees his ministerial duty as 'not important' (p. 60). He uses the time he should have devoted to the speech he is to deliver at the first book exhibition of works by local authors in a trip to the hospital to pick up girls. He demonstrates total ignorance concerning the famous novel written by the president of the writers' association. He does not recognize the difference between creative writers and others. He publicly mentions both Shakespeare and Michael West as creative writers. His concern in the coming election is not with what he has achieved but that his people should return him unopposed. He tries to bribe Odili with money and scholarship to get him to step down in his favour. He sees politics as a dirty game, and concludes that it should be left to people like him, 'who know how to play it' (p. 119).

When Chief Nanga's attempt to bribe Odili to step down fails he resorts to arm-twisting methods. He arranges for Odili to lose his job, and sees to it that he is mercilessly beaten up and framed for being in possession of dangerous weapons, a ploy to prevent him from signing his nomination paper for the election. Even Odili's father is not spared; he is removed as local chairman and his pension tax inflated. Max, the intellectual leader of C.P.C., is killed by Chief Koko's (his political opponent) jeep as he tries to investigate the information on election malpractice being carried out by Chief Koko's supporters.

Given this level of commitment to government affairs, officials find it difficult to support the government policy, as revealed in the coffee saga in Chief Koko's house. In spite of the fact that government has mounted a gigantic campaign to promote 'OHMS – Our Home Made Stuff' (p. 35), Chief Koko still takes imported Nescafé. On the sole occasion his cook brewed the locally processed coffee for the minister, he accused the cook of poisoning his coffee. Apparently the government campaign urging 'every patriot to support this great national effort which ... held the key to economic emancipation without which our hard-won political freedom was a mirage' (p. 35) is not meant for government officials. Mrs Nanga's description of the talk of people in authority as 'nine pence talk and three pence food ... All na lie lie' (p. 36) is entirely accurate.

Nkwelle Ekaney (1980: 114) sees *AMOP* as representing Achebe's 'unmistakable concern for the selfishness, avarice and misrule of political power and positions by many politicians of the newly-independent African states'. Achebe himself, commenting (1983: 1) on the role leaders play in maintaining a healthy political system in Nigeria, notes that 'the Nigerian problem is the unwillingness or inability of its leaders to rise to the responsibility, to the challenge of personal example which are the hallmarks of true leadership'.

Even the intelligent new breed of politicians as represented by Odili and Max are also not committed to their ideals. Odili's political ambition is born out of a personal desire to take Edna from Chief Nanga. When that appears to have failed 'a thought sneaked into my mind and told me it was futile now to try and go through with my political plans' (p. 130). Max justifies his collecting money from Chief Koko on the grounds that P.O.P. is founded by external forces and as such there is no way 'to fight such a dirty war without soiling your hands a little' (p. 126). He also tells Odili's people to support Odili not because of merit but because 'a goat does not eat into a hen's stomach no matter how friendly the two may be' (p. 125).

Irrespective of Odili's description of Chief Nanga as 'bush' and 'you call yourself Minister of Culture' (p. 72) and Max's verdict that the political situation is what it is because intelligent people leave politics to illiterates like Chief Nanga (p. 76), there does not appear to be any appreciable difference between their conduct and Chief Nanga's. Like Chief Nanga they accept the corrupt influence of money in politics. Also like Chief Nanga, Odili accepts the amoral situation in the country and tries to make the best of it. Thus, far from standing outside the corruption that has engulfed the political system and demonstrating a high degree of commitment towards restoring political sanity, the intellectuals are very much a part of the problem.

And yet commitment is crucial if any meaningful political progress is to be achieved. The success recorded by the colonialist is a consequence of total involvement in the colonial mission, however reprehensible. According to Achebe: 'The builders of empire who turned me into a "British protected person" knew the importance of being earnest ... it seems to me obvious that if I desire to change the role and identity fashioned for me by those earnest agents of colonialism I will need to borrow some of their resolve.'[6]

To bring about political development, therefore, there is a need for African leaders to 'borrow' some of the colonialist 'resolve' by showing a total sense of commitment to the demands of their office.

Ngugi also sees political development as hindered by leaders who do not have the commitment of the people as their priority. In *TRB*, Kabonyi in his bid to project himself as the leader Mugo prophesied about and possibly also to secure the position for his son, Kamau, uses his office as the leader of the Kiama to destroy Waiyaki. This action robs the people of a visionary leader who might have been able to unite the people to put up the kind of resistance needed to protect their land from the white man's invasion.

Like the leaders in *AMOP*, the MP representing Gikonyo's district in Ngugi's *AGOW* sees his office solely as a means of amassing wealth. Instead of helping Gikonyo and other farmers to obtain a loan to buy a farm, he double-crosses them and acquires the farm for himself. And this after Gikonyo has made several trips to Nairobi to see him on the subject of the loan. Like most MPs he does not have an office in his constituency. What does this reveal about his level of contact with his people, his understanding of their problems and needs?

In *DOTC* the workers' garage is sold by the city council to 'Boss Kihara and a group of foreigners from USA, Germany and Japan' (p. 223) so as to set up a big tourist hotel to promote 'modern prostitution' (p. 223). This in spite of the fact that the workers have already informed the city council of their ambition to build a modern communally owned garage on the site.

Citizenship *NLAE* deals with the people's expectations of their leaders. Obi's fall is not seen by the people as portending ill but rather as an inability to apply the correct rules of the game: 'Obi tried to do what everyone does without finding out how it was done' (p. 5). Indeed, he is *expected* to take bribe. Joseph's colleague takes it for granted that as secretary of the scholarship board Obi 'go make plenty money there. Every student who wan go England go de see am for house' (p. 70). This, of course, turns out to be correct as the cases of Miss Mark and others demonstrate. It is equally instructive that the only question one of the members of the panel interviewing Obi asks is, 'Why do you want a job in the civil service? So that you can take bribe?' (p. 36).

AMOP also suggests that those people's attitudes to politics and political situations are partly responsible for the irresponsible conduct of their leaders and the consequent lack of political progress. Although Odili knows how Chief Nanga became a minister and how corrupt he is, he readily accepts his invitation to stay with him in Bori. Instead he wonders if, perhaps, he 'had been applying to politics stringent standards that didn't belong to it' (p. 9). And he is quite comfortable about going on a womanizing jamboree with Chief Nanga until he takes Elsie from him.

Odili also reveals that the people who came to listen to Chief Nanga during his inaugural campaign meeting know that he is an 'Honourable Thief'! (p. 138). Telling them will only attract laughter and comments such as 'What a fool! Was he not here when white men were eating?' (p. 138). The masses see nothing wrong with their leaders following the white man's example, but they fail to question the details of that example. Why doesn't Chief Nanga, for instance, emulate Mr Green's devotion to duty in *NLAE*? Obi admits that, rain or shine, Mr Green 'was in the office half an hour before the official time, and quite often worked long after two, or returned again in the evening' (p. 96).

In addition, his audience greets Max's account of the swindle and corruption committed by government officials with 'the laughter of resignation to misfortune' (p. 123). For although 'they understood what was being said', and 'had seen it with their own eyes, what did anyone expect them to do?' (p. 124).

This resignation is reminiscent of Obierika's account in *TFA* as regards the reason the war-loving people of Umuofia find it difficult to fight the white man. Having won some Umuofians, the clan could no longer act as one and so was powerless to stop the erosion of its political system. Even after independence, people continued to regard politics as a white man's affair. Edna's mother's response, when her husband tells her that Odili is challenging Chief Nanga in the parliamentary election, is pertinent, 'What is my share in that? They are both white man's people. And they know what is what between themselves. What do we know?' (p. 106).

Indeed: what *do* the common people know? Chief Nanga finds it easy to order the pipes delivered for the Urua water project to be removed and some of them redelivered after the villagers publicly denounce their own son in order to support him because the villagers consider the government's gesture as a favour and not a right. Instead, in response to the accusation levelled against the government by Max, the ex-policeman tells his people, 'We know they are eating but we are eating too. They are bringing us water and they promise to bring us electricity' (p. 124). Government is seen as doing the people a favour by performing its functions. Achebe draws attention to this attitude (1983: 24) when he asserts that 'the politician may pay them [the masses] a siren-visit once in four years and promise to *give* them this and that and the other. He never says that what he *gives* is theirs in the first place.'

It is this state of affairs that makes it possible for ministers to live in 'cosy comfort of a princely seven bathroom mansion with its seven gleaming, silent action water closets!' (pp. 40–1). The masses, on the other hand, use pails for their excrement and share a room with bags of rice, garri, beans and other foodstuffs and, of course, the rats. Small wonder that the masses see the mainspring of political action as personal gain. Odili's father is satisfied with what Odili has got out of his new party, especially the car. At no point does he question his son's object in venturing into politics.

Of all that is said during the launching of the C.P.C. campaign, the only word that both 'entered' and 'built' a house in the ears of an elderly local councillor is that 'our own son should go and bring our share' (p. 125). This is, of course, received with 'great applause from the crowd' (p. 125). The issue of whether Odili is qualified for the post or even has a sincere interest in it is not considered important. Odili admits that his political plans have always been a little nebulous. And although his self-analysis cannot produce any answer to the question 'how important was my political activity in its own right' (p. 108), his people's interest is in their son obtaining their own share by whatever means. Thus, rather than act as a check on the political excesses of their leaders, the masses are content with the emergence of a country in which the most corrective force is 'you chop, me sef I chop, palaver finish' (p. 161), and where men of worth can easily forget what they said yesterday. Yet without the willingness of the citizens, rulers' power cannot become sacrosanct.

Ngugi sees the people's role as decisive in determining the conduct of leaders and the kind of society they rule. Kenya's independence is to a great extent made possible because the people take up arms in *WNC* and *AGOW* against the colonial government.

In *AGOW* the cashier of the bus Gikonyo boarded to Nairobi after bribing the African policemen that stopped them for overloading tells the passengers that 'they just wanted a few shillings for tea' (p. 54). This is greeted by laughter from the people in the bus. Where this kind of attitude prevails it is little wonder that the people, after travelling from their villages to see their MPs in Nairobi, are willing to 'keep on coming, day after day, without seeing their representative' (p. 54). When they come at all, as in the case of Gikonyo's MP, he can calmly go into his office 'without apologising' (p. 55), even though people have been waiting for him for hours. Although Gikonyo 'was slightly bitter about having to go all the way to Nairobi' (p. 53) to see his MP, who should have had an office in his constituency, he keeps his resentment to himself. Instead, he agrees to carry the MP's message that he cannot come for the Uhuru celebrations organized in his constituency because he has other functions to attend. And when Gikonyo discovers that the MP has swindled him and his friends, he goes home to vent his frustration on his wife instead of going to confront the MP.

In *DOTC* the influential people see self-government as an avenue to strengthening their relationship with foreigners who can teach them how to rob and ruin the country's economy and destabilize the political system. They openly hold a competition to select seven experts in modern theft and robbery with the support of their foreign patrons. The only competitor who opposes the idea of robbing the country in conjunction with foreigners is killed after the contest to pacify the foreign delegates. The resistance of the workers, peasants, petty traders and students, however, is able to stop the competition and chase away the robbers and their foreign patrons. The political message here is unmistakable: ultimately the power to transform society lies with the people.

All in all, the political import of the works examined is evident in the way they expose different systems of political arrangements, beliefs and practices. The reader is invited to evaluate the issues raised. And since the novels are so eloquent, the reader's judgement will, invariably, be of a high critical standard. The reader's understanding of the political issues raised and, most probably, his or her worldview will be influenced. The ideas contained in these works can assist the reader's understanding of African political issues. Indeed, C. L. Innes (1990: 1) asserts that Achebe's 'novels and critical pronouncements have profoundly influenced his readers' understanding of Africans and their lives'. Achebe himself is of the view that an African creative writer must pursue 'right and just causes' in his society, confront 'the big social and political issues of contemporary Africa' if he or she is not to end up like 'that absurd man in the proverb who leaves his burning house to pursue a rat fleeing from flames'.[7] Ngugi (1972: xvi), equally, sees literature as 'what any political and economic arrangement does to the spirit governing human relationship'. Innes, in fact, also maintains (1990: 19–20) that for Ngugi 'the colonial encounter, the tension between African and Western cultures and values, and the emphasis on the novel as a means of political understanding and change are central'. Jude Agho (1995: 107) also commends Ngugi for his ability to fuse the 'artistic' with the 'political'.

It is clear that Achebe and Ngugi qualify to be considered as political thinkers.

FOUR

Achebe's reformist agenda in *Anthills of the Savannah*

§ *Anthills of the Savannah* (Achebe 1987), more than any other of Achebe's works, attempts to explore Africa's contemporary political situation. The question of the involvement of the military in African politics is discussed. The reasons why military governments ultimately fail are provided. The issue of the purpose of political power is explored. The implications of its use or abuse for achieving a genuine liberation are explained. And the ideology most likely to reorder contemporary African societies successfully is suggested.

Plot

The political condition in Africa is portrayed through events in Kangan, a fictional African state. In Achebe's story, the military have just assumed power after ousting a corrupt and incompetent civilian administration. As far as the people are concerned, the removal of the civilian government is well deserved; 'our civilian politicians finally got what they had coming to them and landed unloved and unmourned on the rubbish heap' (p. 12). *Anthills* suggests that it is the corrupt nature of the politics practised by civilian politicians that brought about military intervention, which is expected to embark on a programme to restore order.

This, however, is not to be. Young army officers execute the coup that ousts the civilians from power. Beyond the immediate need to take over the reins of government, the young coup-makers have no articulated programme of action. *Anthills* sees this directionlessness as an inherent character of military takeovers. The way coups are brought about makes them difficult to prepare properly, given that they are normally secret affairs and usually executed as quickly as possible to maintain secrecy. The hasty nature of coup-making makes it difficult for good leaders to emerge, because proper leadership entails a detailed and articulated plan of action; defined ideology or ideologies; modalities for effecting structural changes where necessary; and open deliberation involving civil society.

All the coup-makers can do is invite a young army commander,

Sam, who has 'pretty few ideas about what to do' to become 'His Excellency the Head of State' (p. 12). 'Without any preparation for political leadership', His Excellency turns to his friends for advice. His Executive Council members are recruited on the advice of friends; there is no screening exercise to determine their qualifications, and invariably, those obtaining public office see themselves as indebted to His Excellency. This turns them into 'yes-men' and makes opposition unlikely in the event of His Excellency stepping out of line. More importantly, without preparation on the part of His Excellency and no objective criteria applied for recruiting cabinet members, there is no shared vision among the leaders.

The outcome is that the cabinet members supposed to be 'the cream of our society and the hope of the black race' (p. 2) turn out to be spineless, visionless men who resort to boot-licking and even back-biting to remain in His Excellency's favour. They refuse to see (or, to be more accurate, cannot act) the crucial role they are called upon to play in turning society around. Although there is clear opposition to Sam's bid to become life-president, the Commissioner for Justice and Attorney-General tells him that 'the people have spoken. Their desire is manifest. You are condemned to serve them for life' (p. 5). This is loudly applauded by the other cabinet members. Given this kind of attitude from those entrusted with the responsibility of protecting citizens from power abuse and excesses of leaders, His Excellency assumes absolute power. There is now only one way for society to go: downwards.

The refusal of the drought-stricken province of Abazon to endorse His Excellency's bid to become president-for-life earns it a work-stop order on its borehole project to show the province 'what it means to offend the sun' (p. 127). He utilizes every opportunity to reduce his cabinet members to his victims, like a lion taming a leopard (p. 22). He sees them as a 'no Executive Council' (p. 19). He sets up secret police, the state Research Council, to silence political opponents and dissenters; 'there were unconfirmed rumours of unrest, secret trials and executions in the barracks' (p. 14). Ikem Osodi, the poet-journalist, is cold-bloodedly murdered because of his crusading editorials and criticisms of the government's excesses. Christopher Oriko (Chris), the Commissioner of Information, who dares expose the complicity of the government in Ikem's death, is hounded out of the state capital, Bassa, to a remote village where he is killed. The general political atmosphere is characterized by arbitrary use of power – 'worshipping a dictator is such a pain in the ass' but 'the real problem is having no way of knowing from one day to another, from one minute to the next, just what is up and what is down' (p. 45).

Anthills describes the authoritarian character of military regimes, with their lack of concern for people's wellbeing a major cause of alienation between government and civil society. The oppressive character of the military regime does not elicit a feeling of belonging to the state from the people. Since they have not taken part in the selection of the leaders, and are not in a position to influence government policies, the people see themselves as outsiders in state matters. Economically, the people are also not integrated into government affairs. Given that the military both control power and possess the instrument to silence any form of opposition, they openly loot the nation's treasury (p. 42) without concern for people's welfare.

Achebe's position is that it is the leaders, primarily, who can remedy this situation. They deserve blame for whatever political condition exists. No system of government is inherently bad; rather, it is individuals who order the society and can consequently make it good or bad. In *The Trouble with Nigeria*, Achebe avers (1983: 1) that the 'trouble with Nigeria is simply and squarely a failure of leadership'. The leaders' inability to act as role models is presented as the single most important factor blocking political progress. By engaging in a celebration of indiscipline, the leaders can only inspire the people to wanton acts of misconduct, cruelty, greed, corruption and other anti-social vices that make it impossible to maintain a healthy polity. The old man from Abazon reminds us that it is the leaders who hold both 'the yam and the knife' (p. 127).

In spite of the blame placed on the leaders, *Anthills* suggests that the attitude of the people to political events also plays some role in determining the political climate in the country. The complacent attitude of the people to the coup, their mindless rejoicing at every change of government, make coups attractive to plotters. It will take His Excellency's ruthless programme of intimidation, torture, cold-blooded murder, terrorism, gross economic mismanagement and his own brutal slaying for the 'gullible people of Kangan, famous for dancing in the streets at every change of government' (p. 218) to begin to ask questions.

The corruption of civil servants and students is also highlighted as a brake on political progress. Workers and students connive with government, through their self-serving attitudes, to destabilize and decivilize society. Instead of presenting articulated opposition to the military's oppressive regime, the workers embezzle millions, protest over irrelevant issues – the national president at an all-Africa congress refuses to leave his hotel room until an official Peugeot 504 assigned to him is replaced with a Mercedes – go on strike to protect outdated and outrageous colonial privileges such as motor vehicle advances and allowances, and condone absenteeism, ghost workers and scandalously low national productivity (p. 157). The students engage in destruction of public facilities, and intensify religious and tribal conflicts.

Indeed, the privileged few see the masses as 'not in the least like ourselves. They don't need and can't use the luxuries that you and I must have. They have the animal capacity to endure the pain of … domestication' (p. 40). One can almost hear Lugard (1968: 309) proclaiming the Africans savages who do not think or act as Europeans do. Africans 'in truth', are like 'dumb driven cattle'.

Even the down-trodden are not spared in this indictment. The masses who come to witness the execution of the four armed robbers laugh 'blatantly at their own humiliation and murder' (p. 42). They fail to see that the robbers are micro-images of 'leaders who openly looted our treasury, whose effrontery soiled our national soul' (p. 42). Instead they have become so desensitized that even if their mother were to be held by 'her legs and torn down the middle like a piece of old rag that crowd would have yelled with eye-watering laughter' (p. 42).

The attitude of the two taxi-drivers who call on Ikem to apologize for the conduct of one of them in contending for a place in the traffic queue with Ikem reveals how the masses endorse their condition. The taxi-driver blames his conduct on Ikem driving 'a battered old Datsun instead of a Mercedes and for driving with his own hands instead of sitting in the owner's corner and being driven' (p. 138). The abdication of responsibility by civil society and their active collaboration in keeping society oppressed emphasizes the importance of having good leaders. The people's conduct is showcased to expose the degree of depravity society suffers when it does not receive good and adequate nourishment from its leaders.

From whatever angle the problem of Africa's political predicament is approached, *Anthills*'s position is that good leadership is crucial. The military has failed, just as their civilian counterparts did, to restore order and impose economic discipline. By the end of the story, the sad truth is revealed: nothing has really changed with the military takeover. Things may have got worse. Anything can, still, literally go on in Kangan: chaotic billing procedures deliberately designed to cover massive fraud; the burning of entire accounts and audit departments to prevent inquiry; bribery on the highways; inexplicable traffic jams; the brutality of law enforcement officers; secret executions in barracks and open murder on the road; the shooting of striking railway workers and demonstrating students and the destruction and banning of independent unions and co-operatives; unproductive cabinet meetings; subservience to foreign manipulation; second-class, hand-me-down capitalism; the absence of a national ethos; inordinate ambition to hang on to power; social injustice and the elevation of the cult of mediocrity.

Public office-holders use their positions to privatize public wealth and resources. His Excellency is believed to have acquired eight ocean liners, two or three private jets, a private jetty for smuggling, fifty-odd companies including a bank, a monopoly of government fertilizer imports (p. 117) through a front man. Millions are still squandered on 'irresponsibly extravagant' projects. The presidential retreat, built by the civilian government at a cost of forty-five million, is refurbished by the military with twenty million, which does not pass 'through the normal Ministry of Finance procedures' (p. 73). The presidential retreat functions as a wall to separate the government 'from the people and their basic needs of water which is free from Guinea worm, of simple shelter and food' (p. 73).

Ikem, who embodies the message of Achebe's political ideology, sees the prime failure of government as its inability to 're-establish vital inner links with the poor and dispossessed of this country, with the bruised heart that throbs painfully at the core of the nation's being' (p. 141). Leaders who have the will, the ability and the vision to embark on a well-conceived and consistent agenda of reform are required. According to Ikem, reform offers 'the most promising route to success in the real world' (p. 99). It is necessary at this point to investigate what informs this ideological perspective and to assess its adequacy as the ideology of social change in Africa.

Reformist agenda: 'no' to the one-solution approach

Reform has the capacity to accommodate differences and contradictions, necessary preconditions in the search for creative solutions. Given the African situation, in which the political culture of most countries is characterized by differences (often irreconcilable) in religious beliefs, ideological leaning, moral doctrines and economic outlook, it is often difficult to get the people to engage in coherent, collective endeavours or even freely to endorse a common political regime. It is important to avoid an ideology that is orthodox in character, discourages contradictions and thus is more likely to ignite the tension already existing in most African states. Nigeria, for instance, is an artificial political construct and the 1914 amalgamation of the country's northern and southern parts did nothing to address the incompatibility between the two sections in terms of their culture, vision and outlook.

Ikem sees an orthodox ideology, such as ushering in a revolution to institute a proletarian government as the grand solution to all African problems, as incapable of conferring the kind of freedom necessary for the achievement of an enduring political transformation. Ikem's rejection of the idea of revolution stems from the combination of at least seven ideas.

First, there is no solidarity characterizing the oppressed. The assumption that there is an umbrella body uniting them has no basis in reality. For one thing, the oppressed belong to different groups: workers, peasants, the poor, the unemployed, and even students. The way they perceive oppression is therefore disparate. A worker may be interested in better pay, a peasant in a loan to improve production, the poor in a social welfare package, the unemployed in a job, and a student in good grades that will enable him or her to get a good job. Without a common starting point and a common goal it may be difficult for the oppressed to form a united front.

Again, the oppressed in developed economies may view oppression differently from the oppressed in a developing one. Even differences in residential areas, for instance the urban–rural gap, can affect the responses of the oppressed to their oppression. Writing on Africa, Ben Turok (1987: 92) tells us that 'many writers hold that the peasantry cannot identify with urban workers because of blatant inequalities between them'. The assumption, then, that class antagonism is inevitable as implied in the bonding of the oppressed to fight their oppressors, may not be tenable. There may indeed be mutual antagonism in the ranks of the oppressed.

There is no discernible universal pattern across the world, or even in individual countries. In Africa, the working class in countries where large white settler populations existed (South Africa, Zimbabwe and Algeria) is stronger than in most other African countries, due to higher industrial and agricultural development. Vicky Randall and Robin Theobald (1985: 182) have questioned whether class analysis contributes much to our understanding of politics, even in the most industrialized society in the world, the USA. They further note that, in most Third World societies, only a small minority is regularly employed in wage labour, and an even smaller proportion are members of trades unions and other class-based organizations.

In addition, the working-class interest in overthrowing capital is not based on any more worthy ethical consideration than that of motivating capital. The working class coming to a conscious realization of itself as a group that can represent the common interests of humanity is based on material consciousness. Its interest in the revolutionary overthrow of capital, therefore, is purely interest-motivated, just as the owners of production strive to protect their self-interest by exploiting labour.

It is too simplistic, moreover, to view political changes in terms of the oppressed and the oppressor. Other factors such as ethnicity, ideology, religion and even language can (and do) play vital roles. Robert Daniels (1997: 390) sees the factual weaknesses in Marxism as centring on the analysis of classes and the prediction of their future development. He asserts 'the scheme of rulers and exploited is much too simple for any period of history'. It has also been observed (Oguejiofor 2000) that political conflicts in Africa are rooted in ethnic and sectional interest.

Ikem's point here is that a worldwide proletarian revolution is not necessary, or at best is 'a grand illusion'. This is because man's free spirit makes him unpredictable, and 'no system can change that' (p. 99). The best that can be hoped for is an ideology that will confer freedom and allow contradictions, so that different African countries can identify what will work best in ensuring social justice and a healthy living and working environment for their peoples.

Second, even if the revolution succeeds, new oppressors may well spring from among the oppressed. History has revealed that revolutionary governments tend to be despotic. Stalin's USSR, for instance, was characterized by a harsh, repressive system of administration. The Cuba of Batista witnessed unbridled dictatorial power. Robert Nisbet (1982: 267) is of the opinion that 'without exception the revolutionary orders that have replaced old orders have proved far more repressive, despotic, and terroristic than what preceded them'. Robert Daniels (1997: 390) reports that some Marxist writers have suggested that 'the bureaucracy of the communist party has become a new ruling class, which exploits the masses not through private property but through its control of the state'.

Ikem's position is that there is a need for a more rigorous analysis than suggested by the simplistic notion that all problems will melt away once the oppressor has been overthrown by the oppressed. To appreciate Ikem's view, all we need to do is to reflect on this question: does being oppressed imbue one with a fundamental sense of justice and fair play?

Third, experience and intelligence show that mankind's progress in freedom will be piecemeal, slow and undramatic. Experience has shown that communities founded on revolution are frail and evanescent. Revolutionists by their action-oriented character are likely not to have a clear plan about how to proceed once the revolution has succeeded. Robert Daniels (ibid.: 391) discloses that Lenin's anarchistic ideal of state and revolution – the establishment of the dictatorship of the proletariat, equality under the new regime, the withering away of the state – was violated by Lenin himself soon after he took power by his setting up of 'a highly centralized dictatorship and industrial administration'. Indeed, Daniels further reveals (ibid.) that Lenin, shortly before his death in 1924, acknowledged 'that Soviet Russia lacked the economic and cultural foundation for communism' and so, 'a long period of gradual building under the tutelage of the communist party would be necessary'.

Ikem's concern is to sound a warning note, especially in the face of the drive towards modernization by African states. Modernization should be seen as a lengthy process, requiring an evolutionary change rather than a revolutionary one, so that enduring structures can be put in place.

Fourth, the peasants who should form the bulk of the proletariat are often excluded from discussion and decisions regarding government affairs. How can the so-called peasant–worker alliance work if, as revealed during Ikem's lecture at the University of Bassa, the peasants are more engrossed with their struggle for daily survival than in taking over power? Without knowledge of the issues, how are the peasants supposed to represent their own interest? In what way, then, will their situation be better under a revolutionary government? Ikem cautions against the working class imposing its view on the peasants and using them to achieve their ambitions.

Fifth, the workers supposed to be members of the oppressed class are themselves their worst oppressors. Oppression is more multi-faceted than the simple notion of an employer – the oppressor – exploiting an employee – the oppressed. It is also possible that the oppressed can oppress the employer by deliberately working below their capacity. Civil servants are known for preferring to remain under-employed and yet insisting on their full wage. Even when they go on strike (a frequent occurrence in Nigeria, where ASUU, NASU, the transport union, medical doctors, nurses and even the police strike) they still expect (and, in fact, receive) full payment. *Anthills* portrays how civil servants and urban employees of public corporations engage in all forms of vices, ranging from going on strike over flimsy and antiquated colonial privileges to presiding over the sabotage of the nation through unproductivity and fraud. These factors all adversely affect national development.

What Ikem wishes to convey here is the need to recognize that oppressed and oppressor are two sides of the same coin. The distinction between them may not thus be very helpful in the search for a solution to Africa's political situation.

Sixth, students have not been able to rise above a low level of consciousness. The much-vaunted notion of students as future leaders will amount to nothing if the students do not take their responsibility, to point society in the right direction, seriously. As it is, students are no better than the leaders and the oppressors they are supposed to be fighting. They negate the benefits of modern life by taking active part in tribalism, religious extremism, electoral mechandising, destruction of public facilities and by encouraging mediocrity in school and, by extension, in all spheres of life. For students to assume a good moral position from which to criticize their leaders, they have to purge themselves first of their own vices. Ikem's position is that a class war is not as important as serious self-examination; it is this that will, ultimately, lead to the nation's redemption.

Seventh, and last, revolutions are betrayed just as much by stupidity, incompetence, impatience and precipitate action as by inaction. Regarding revolution as a panacea is likely to lead to hasty action. A revolution by itself may not provide the solution if other crucial skills – such as proficiency in the art of governance, competence in leadership, a well-designed education enabling people to understand and implement a new way of life – that really take time to develop are not given a long maturation period.

It is these skills that will bring about a reordering of the society and not a revolution as such. Ikem's view is that it is necessary to make this distinction. What African societies need is an agenda that will bring about the much-needed genuine transformation. Revolution, by its over-emphasis on action, is likely to be hasty and is thus unlikely to produce a lasting, worthwhile result.

It is a combination of these seven ideas that prompts Ikem to reject the idea of revolution. It also leads him to the realization that systems are, perhaps, not what is important. Man's basic capacity for nobility as well as for villainy cannot be changed by any system. What is required is a good spread of general political experience, slow of growth and obstinately patient like David Diop's 'Africa'. The choice of slow reform is not a valid excuse for political inactivity or apathy; rather, it is an insurance against 'false hopes and virulent epidemics of gullibility' (p. 100). What is needed is a new political creed – a 'new radicalism' that is 'clear-eyed' and thoughtful enough to recognize the aforementioned problems so as 'to see beyond the present claptrap that will heap all our problems on the doorstep of capitalism and imperialism' (p. 158).

New radicalism: a welcome panacea

The 'New Radicalism' aims at specific objectives. There is opposition to the dependency-school view that sees all Africa's problem of underdevelopment as imposed from outside – specifically, by imperialist capitalist economies. This position is that it is the owners of international capital that control African affairs, be they political, economic, or social. The greatest hindrances to national development in African states, then, are the perpetuation of unequal exchange and the historical legacy of colonialism.

The characteristic feature of colonialism is the subordinate relationship it introduced between the West and Africa. This is especially manifest in the unequal economic exchange that it engendered, resulting in the division of the global economy into two: the 'core' (the West) and the 'periphery' (African states and other Third World economies). Claude Ake (2001: 18) observes that 'it would have been difficult for African countries to avoid dependent development because of the integration of African economies into the metropolitan economies during the colonial era'. Unfortunately, even independence has not been able to reverse this situation. The West, by virtue of its industrial, technological, military, economic and political advancement is still able to manipulate African states.

Anthills, however, questions the adequacy of this explanation in accounting for Africa's contemporary condition. Ikem argues that overemphasis on external factors prevents a clear analysis of the problems obstructing Africa's development. As far as he is concerned, these problems are more internal than external. For instance, the activities of civil servants, urban employees of public corporations and students, contribute more in maintaining underdevelopment in African societies than do external factors. For Africa to achieve meaningful development, these internal hindrances have to be addressed first. With a good foundation it will be easier to tackle external factors. Indeed, African leaders are waking up to the fact that Africa's problems and the solutions to them have to be sought internally. Chris Simpson (2002: 39) reports that the main selling point of the New Partnership for Africa's Development (Nepad), started by the presidents of Nigeria, South Africa, Senegal and Algeria, has been 'its emphasis on African "ownership" of Africa's problems and solutions'. (It is, however, still too early to judge their commitment and Nepad's success.)

Ikem's position is that by focusing on dependency, distinction between the core and periphery, exploiters and exploited, adequate analyses of variations in economic resource base, potential for development, demographic composition, socio-political structure and specific trends peculiar to different African states will be obscured. Immanuel Wallerstein argues, rightly, that the world is too complicated to be classified as a bimodal system, with cores and peripheries only.[1] Also, dependency does not allow for a variety of choices in the search for a solution; it cannot act as an adequate guide to the understanding of the complexities of Africa's political predicament. What Africa needs is an ideology that encourages analytic growth, not one that forecloses further inquiry and presents political conflict and outcome in static terms.

There is also a rejection of the notion that the military might be agents of modernization in Africa, which was a common view among social scientist in the 1960s. Vicky Randall and Robin Theobald (1985: 74) quote Halpern as stating that 'in civilian politics corruption, nepotism and bribery loomed much larger'. Whereas, 'within the army a sense of national mission transcending parochial, regional or economic interests or kinship ties seemed to be much more clearly defined than anywhere else in society'. Ernest E. Lefever is even more extreme in his opinion (1970: 21). He sees African armies as tending to be the most 'detribalised, westernised, modernised, integrated and cohesive institutions in their respective states'. He goes on to assert that 'the army is usually the most disciplined agency in the state' and states: 'a more vivid symbol of sovereignty than the flag, the constitution, or the parliament, the army often evokes more popular sentiment than a political leader'.

Anthills questions the myth that portrays the military as a class set apart from society which can transcend the conflicts – corruption, bribery, nepotism – of civilian politics. A good deal of evidence indicates that the ills that plague civilian politics are equally present within the military. Where the civil administration has spent only forty-five million to build the presidential retreat, the military that ousted them from power to save the country from corruption, used twenty million to refurbish it. The drought-stricken Abazonians are denied their share of national resources because they refused to support His Excellency's bid to become life president. Citizens' rights are trampled upon with impunity. Ikem is murdered for his critical opinions of the military's excesses.

These events are no different from happenings under the military administration in Africa. In Nigeria, for instance, the regimes of

Babangida and Abacha were characterized by unbridled violence, looting of the economy and the entrenchment of draconian policies. Throughout their reigns there were rumours of unrest, open and secret trials and executions. Any form of opposition constituted a virtual invitation to be killed. Dele Giwa, the ex-editor of *Newswatch* magazine, was killed during the Babangida regime because it was believed that he had some explosive information on the government. Kudirat Abiola, Pa Rewane, Ken Saro Wiwa, to mention just a few, were also murdered for their criticism of the Abacha government. The present federal government of Obasanjo is still trying to recover some of Abacha's 'loot' stashed away in foreign banks. Before his death in 1998, Abacha was engaged in a bid to transform himself into a life-president.

Those who cannot withstand the rigour of brutal intimidation or possible death become puppets, sycophants and imitators of the military dictators. There were many expensive campaign adverts to support Abacha's bid to transform himself from a military head of state to a civilian life-president. The two-million-man march and 'Youth Ask Earnestly for Abacha' movement are cases in point. The law-enforcement officers, as imitators of their masters, intimidate and shoot innocent citizens. A bus-driver or a bus conductor can be killed for no other reason than not giving *egunje* (bribes) to a traffic police-man. The result is that society simmers in corruption and indiscipline. The military, therefore, has not been more effective than its civilian counterparts in bringing development. Indeed, Ezenwa-Ohaeto (1997: 243) quotes Achebe in an interview he granted to Okey Ndibe and C. Don Adinuba for the *African Guardian* in 1985 as saying that 'military regimes are part of the problem of Africa, part of the problem of underdevelopment; of foreign control, of irresponsible leadership, of interference by the major powers. Africa is caught in all these problems and therefore Africa is unstable. Military regimes occur as an indication of the in-built instability in African nations at this time in their history.'

It is vital to identify the factors that make it possible for the wrong people to get into key positions. The interest of the colonial masters at the time of granting independence to African states was in ensuring that they, the masters, retained the exploitative economic hold they had on Africa. They therefore tried their best to ensure that the Africans that succeeded them were 'yes-men' they could control. Given that colonial rule was founded on oppression and dispossession and betrayed no interest whatsoever in nation-building, these successors were encouraged to follow the same path. The result is that the independence of African states came without concomitant economic, financial and ideological freedoms. Instead of political independence, African states found themselves in a new colonial situation: neo-colonialism.

Given the West's economic, military, technological, industrial and political power, it is easy for Westerners to destabilize any African leader who attempts to show vision and ability in directing the affairs of his country and to replace him with a more amenable leader. This scenerio encourages visionless, grossly incompetent leaders to emerge in African states.

Both His Excellency and his cabinet members are depicted as visionless, self-centred and completely unfit leaders who more or less blundered into power. His Excellency's greatest concern is not to be ridiculed in *Time* magazine. It does not matter that his dictatorial decision to stop the water project in Abazon is causing severe hardship to his citizens. He extends himself to play host to the visiting American journalist to the point that she can without any kind of preamble read him and his subjects 'a lecture on the need for the country to maintain its present levels of foreign debt servicing' (p. 78). And he labels Beatrice a 'racist' (p. 81) and ignominiously dismisses her from the party for questioning the appropriateness of his conduct before this journalist.

Anthills details the political problems of Africa – unnecessary intimidation of opponents, complete disregard for law and social justice, useless pandering to the West, among other things – and sees them as obstacles in the way of getting the right calibre of people to lead nations. To reverse this situation there is a need to reorder society. This will involve the full, or at least active, co-operation of all.

By highlighting the need for general political experience, *Anthills* points to the need for widespread participation in politics, which will prevent the concentration of benefits in a few hands. Where electorates are vigilant, the power of those in government is bound to be limited. Conversely, electoral apathy is the best way to encourage bad governance. A good spread of political experience is necessary if a common purpose is to emerge from the discordant voices that clamour for attention in African countries. Deliberation, such as takes place at the end of *Anthills*, provides a platform for citizens to reach agreement on important issues. Beatrice and Emmanuel, the students' union president, reach a consensus that 'people' and 'ideas' are important in bringing about a change in people's orientation and in society as a whole.

The concern with social and economic justice is particularly understandable in the case of Nigeria, with its history of civil war. Emeka Ojukwu (1969: 12) notes that 'without social justice, harmony and stability within society disappear and antagonisms between various sections of the community take their place'. Achebe (1983: 19–25), equally, maintains that social injustice and the cult of mediocrity can ultimately devastate an entire society. In *Anthills*, Ikem observes that 'the real solution lies in a world in which charity will have become unnecessary' (p. 155).

There is, however, a need for caution regarding political fanaticism. In an age where fanaticism in almost all aspects of life – religious, economic, cultural and, especially, political – is becoming common-place, the new radicalism, with its moderate temper, must be seen as a timely ideal. The need for a tolerant society has, possibly, never been as urgent as it is now.

Individual freedom and the safety of society must both be guaranteed. The totalitarian nature inherent in the dictatorship of the proletariat and the institutionalization of communism is bound to stifle individual creativity and, in turn, affect the general wellbeing of society. Equally important is the need to structure society in such a way that there is regard for the rule of law by both the government and its cohorts. A common feature of most African countries is the attitude of the privileged, who feel entitled to live above the law. This enables them to unleash all manner of anti-social behaviour on society. Ezenwa-Ohaeto (1997: 219) quotes Achebe as stating that 'a society which represses the individual spirit will rapidly degenerate into stagnant mediocrity. But without society there can be no meaningful individuality to exercise and no civilization.'

It is important to reorder the political culture through a reorientation of attitude, especially on the part of the leaders. This is crucial because without good governance, the idea of social and economic justice is highly compromised. Society often reflects the kind of leadership in place over it. Where leaders are seen as not performing well, political distrust results. Marc Hetherington (1998: 791) notes, 'low trust helps create a political environment in which it is more difficult for leaders to succeed'. Hetherington also remarks (ibid.: 804) that 'without public support for solutions, problems will linger, will become more acute, and if not resolved will provide the foundation for renewed discontent'.

This focus on leaders notwithstanding, citizens share some responsibility for instituting and maintaining a healthy political culture. Ikem reminds the students at Bassa University that they are in a position to put the nation on the road to self-redemption if they can clean up their act so as to have the moral authority to lecture the national leadership. In *Trouble*, Achebe equally opines (1983: 1–2) that it is the duty of enlightened citizens to lead the way in the discovery of good leaders and to create an atmosphere conducive to their emergence.

There is discernible confusion in the leadership thesis on which *Anthills*'s reformist agenda critically depends. Achebe appears to offer two contradictory criteria for responsible leadership.

'Leader-centrism': a thesis in self-conflict

First, Achebe's argument affirms not just that the question of leadership is paramount but that it is uniquely so. 'The prime failure of this government,' Ikem reflects, 'is the failure of our rulers to re-establish vital inner links with the poor and dispossessed of this country' (p. 141). In *Trouble*, Achebe (1983: 10) insists that Nigerians are what they only because their leaders are *not* what *they* should be.

Second, leaders' inability to live up to the demands of their office is caused by their subjects (the led) not insisting on responsible leadership. Who, then, effectively provides the direction – the leaders or the led? In a situation where the leaders are responsible for the prime failure of the system and the led have the responsibility of making these leaders provide 'responsible performance', which group emerges as the authentic leaders? Or is responsibility equally shared? If so, what is the difference between leaders and the led?

Then, again, there is the suggestion that the elite are best placed to handle (and should, in fact, be left to handle) affairs of state. The account of the happenings in the fictional state of Kangan is given predominantly from the perspective of the elites: Chris, the commissioner for information; Ikem, the editor of the *National Gazette*; and Beatrice, senior assistant secretary in the Ministry of Finance. It is, naturally, one of them, Ikem, that articulates the political message in *Anthills*. And at the end, after Ikem's and Chris's demise, it is Beatrice who becomes 'a captain whose leadership was sharpened more and more by sensitivity to the peculiar needs of her company' (p. 229).

The point is that overemphasis on the elite undermines political participation, a fundamental factor in bringing about genuine liberation in a democratic setting. Moreover, the position that the elites are the best placed to handle the affairs of state is premised on a weak functionalist argument – because the elites know much more than ordinary people and are in position to perform useful functions in society, then they are the best. This position completely neglects the issue of whether the system is truly representative of the common will and free of class or personal interest. The 'loopholes' of elitism are glaring.

Ikem, Chris and Beatrice do not see the masses as having any meaningful contribution to make to political life in the country. It is only when they are faced with danger that they recognize the need for others outside their class to participate. And yet the point to which Achebe wishes to draw attention is the indispensability of experts, as far as is compatible with the need for political equality. Dahl (1998: 78–9) notes that advocates of democratic government have to confront the serious problem of how best to satisfy democratic criteria, maintain a satisfactory degree of political equality and yet rely on experts and expert knowledge in making public decisions.

Also, the system of government in place is not considered important in achieving meaningful reform. But can the proposed solution be achieved without any recourse to systems whatsoever? According to Beatrice, Chris's last words are a message to beware that 'this world belongs to the people of the world not to any little caucus, no matter how talented' (p. 232). And in *Trouble*, Achebe (1983: 25) insists that 'the masses own the nation because they have the number'. Yet there is no indication that the masses want anything to do with the leadership. If anything, they seem indifferent to their oppression. The crowd at the execution ground 'laughed so blatantly at their own humiliation and murder' (p. 41). The taxi-driver's excuse for mistaking Ikem for some 'jajajaja' person is because Ikem's car is 'too old' and Ikem is driving it himself. In fact, Ikem is condemned for not turning himself into a 'master'. Also, all Elewa's uncle asks for is to be included in the plans of the elites. The idea that he should take part in making the plan appears preposterous to him. He cannot conceive of living in a house like Beatrice's. The best he can ask for is to be allowed to visit again.

Even the old man, from the rebellious Abazon, who understands the need for political opposition, will be satisfied if all they ever achieve is a future generation saying that they tried. He sees their attempt as the puny effort of the tortoise about to be killed by the leopard. How, then, can the people of the world take hold of the world that is said to belong to them?

The issue is not primarily concerned with the system of government, but finding a good leader to act as a role model. And yet *Anthills*'s account shows that becoming a leader and possessing a sense or capacity for social justice are two distinct issues. Indeed, individuals' capacity for social or moral correctness differs. To maintain a standard social code for society there is a need for social institutions to moderate both the conduct of the leaders and of the citizens. *Anthills* suggests that unrestrained exercise of economic rights under a capitalist system engenders serious social divisions and antagonisms. Civilized, political stability demands far-reaching reform – 'The real solution,' Ikem proclaims, 'lies in a world in which charity will have become unnecessary' (p. 115). This, no doubt, implies better distribution of wealth to enhance the welfare of the masses, as opposed to the competition and disregard for citizens' welfare that characterize a capitalist economy. Achebe's reformist agenda, then, has as an ethical guide a social ideal broader than what liberty alone can guarantee. There is an infusion of a socialist concern for community. This challenges and undermines the leader-centric position of *Anthills*. *Anthills* (unwittingly, perhaps) contains the seed of its own destruction.

Besides, in spite of the commitment to freedom that pervades *Anthills*, Achebe is careful not to uphold the unrestrained and uncompromising economic self-interest usually taken as an index of progress in capitalist society. Equally, both the significance of Achebe's ethical vision and the logical coherence of his political thought are determined by his conception of economic justice. *Anthills* seems to suggest that the Lockean possession of whatever one mixes his labour with may not guarantee economic justice. This is because one can use position, rather than labour, to acquire massive wealth. His Excellency, through a front man, has in one year acquired eight ocean liners, two or three private jets, a private jetty, fifty-odd companies, including a bank, monopoly of government fertilizer imports and, of course, automatic clearance for his jetty which is, most likely, used for smuggled goods. Whereas the poor that toil end up possessing nothing, like Elewa's mother, who 'can carry all her worldly wares in one head-load' (p. 156).

Anthills hints that this type of situation hinders the individual's ability to live a life of full civic efficiency. The amount of energy exerted in labour is not in any way porportional to the remuneration citizens receive. Without acceptable and fair remuneration for their labour, most people in society will not be induced to perform at their best. To address this problem requires subtle changes to the system. A healthy reformist agenda cannot afford to neglect the crucial relationship between the political and the economic. Undeniably, the economic affects the political. Under conditions of penury, people are more likely to place themselves in a subservient position and easily yield to any vice, rendering them unwilling to promote the spirit of independence, which is what is needed for political development to take place.

Once more, politics in Africa (as elsewhere) cannot be reduced easily to the activities of leaders. State institutions do not exist in isolation from non-formal structures. The interaction or non-interaction that exists between the two helps determine, shape and direct government action. Power constellations, then, are not entirely leader-centric. The environment, the historical inheritance – colonialism – the relation between the haves and the have-nots, all impose their own constraints.

Lastly, in what way(s) is the 'new radicalism' really new? Its shunning of revolution and advocacy of reform informed by non-violent persistence and stubborn patience is no different from Christ's or Gandhi's political ideal. Its emphasis on the need for political freedom has been the concern of the classical champions of liberty. For Locke, all absolutes in government should be rejected; and although the purpose of government is the preservation of man's property, it should not tamper with it without the individual's consent. The people retain the right to withdraw their allegiance from a government that is not working in their interest.

Conclusion: merits against all odds

These criticisms, however, should not divert attention from Achebe's cardinal points, which are first, to explain that whenever and wherever leaders do not rise to the responsibility of true leadership it is impossible to establish a civil society in which individuals can aspire to their highest potential; and second to show that a violent revolution is neither necessary nor desirable in order to achieve this end.

The aim here is to underscore the fatal threat to which society will be exposed when leaders fail to lead by good example. The first two major threats are, one, that a leader 'has no fellows to restrain him, and the policemen who might have done it are all in his employ' (Achebe 1983: 32). In *Anthills*, a policeman is detailed to convict Ikem on the false allegation of a traffic offence. Second, the immunity enjoyed by a leader as a result of power makes the 'leader the envy of the powerless who will turn him into a role model and imitate his actions of indiscipine' (ibid.). In *Anthills*, an ordinary soldier who nearly killed a young trader due to his reckless driving pointedly tells his near-victim, when he complains, 'if I kill you, I kill Dog' (p. 48). Naturally, the policeman who accosted Ikem with false charges ended his order to Ikem to report to the police station with His Excellency's favourite expression for intimidation 'Kabisa!' (p. 129).

By stressing the importance of leadership, what Achebe wants to draw attention to is that it is individuals who order society and make it good or bad, and not the system itself. Society reflects the quality of leadership in place. The inability of leaders to set good examples produces a society with perverse values, which hinder political progress. Commenting on this in relation to Nigeria, Achebe (ibid.: 10) remarks that, 'to pull her back and turn her around is clearly beyond the contrivance of mediocre leadership. It calls for greatness. Nigerians are what they are only because their leaders are *not* what *they* should be.'

Without good leadership, even a socialist government cannot maintain the political structure. Achebe's concern, therefore, goes beyond systems of government to focus on the key element that will guarantee that the citizens' interest and the safety of the society will be protected whatever system of government is in place. *Anthills*'s success lies in compelling the reader to reflect on this vital issue and decide to what extent the instituting and maintaining of viable political order or reordering of society is more a function of leadership than the structure or system of governance in place. It challenges the reader to look closely at the whole question of revolution and social change and to assess the degree of their continued success in the absence of solid leadership. The solution to the constant changes of government, bloodletting and indisciplined and corrupt citizenry endemic in contemporary African countries cannot, then, lie in the system of government.

Equally, in not supporting revolution, Achebe is trying to avoid the devastation revolution will unleash on the collective psyche if given national backing. Without such backing, violence is daily employed as a means of resolving problems, which it paradoxically ends up exacerbating. The National Association of Nigerian Students, during their election meeting at University of Port Harcourt in March 2002, turned to violence to resolve a political tussle. Some students were killed, others seriously wounded. And, of course, there was no election. In *Anthills*, Ikem indicts the students on the conduct of their colleagues on national service who razed to the ground a new maternity block built by peasants because they were protesting against their posting to a remote rural station without electricity and running water.

The goal in using students as an example is to make the case that if students, who are presumably undergoing training under some supervision and authority in a 'civil' environment, can do these things then it can be easily imagined what activities thugs and other members of a more 'open' society might engage in. In Nigeria, for instance, the violence that occurs almost daily between militant groups, youth organizations, religious fanatics, opposing political parties' supporters, police and armed robbers, would require a study of its own. To give violence the stamp of legitimacy is to extend an invitation for the collapse of civil society, in which case we might as well pack up and return to Hobbes's pre-political enclave. *Anthills*'s insistence that revolution should not be upgraded to a national policy is a recognition of the inherent violent character of modern African states and of the need to protect the individual and the society from it.

Anthills is a statement about the rejection of absolutes in political structures. It advocates the need to take the complex and paradoxical nature of Africa into account in devising political solutions. The reader is compelled to admit that conflicting logic can operate within one universe of discourse as well as provide dialectical advantages. For Achebe, as quoted by Ezenwa-Ohaeto (1997: 254), Africans 'should not be bent on the one-solution approach. Africa is not a one-solution continent. We are not a one-issue continent.' Amen to that.

FIVE
Ngugi's Marxist aesthetics

§ The purpose of this chapter is to investigate a counter-ideology to Achebe's gradual, piecemeal reformist and leader-centric agenda in the search for appropriate social reconstruction of African society. Ngugi's Marxist position in *Petals* is analysed with this in mind. This analysis includes clarifying what Marxist aesthetics is; how it is applicable to Ngugi; and how *Petals* fits into this style of aesthetics.

Marxist aesthetics: a clarification

A point needs to be stated from the outset. Marx has no defined theory on literature. This is not to say that there are no clear indications of his orientation. Marxist aesthetics can be derived from examining statements contained in Marx's and Engels's philosophy.

The core of Marxism can be located in the primacy of matter over mind. For Marx and Engels, economics governs and defines the basis of every relationship. In the 'Manifesto of the Communist Party' Marx and Engels (1968: 51) aver that mankind's consciousness changes with every change in the conditions of material existence, in social relations and social life.

Existence, clearly, precedes consciousness. Mankind's material well-being determines the degree to which individuals can take part in other activities. A person who is hungry, unsheltered and naked will hardly have time to engage in any extra-economic venture. His or her primary concern will be to meet basic needs.

A basic proposition of Marxism is that the economic structure of society, the 'real foundation', is the base, which determines the superstructure – juridical, philosophical, religious, literary, artistic etc. Engels's exposition on this is worth quoting at length.

> Just as Darwin discovered the law of development of organic nature, so Marx discovered the law of development of human history: the simple fact, hitherto concealed by an overgrowth of ideology, that mankind must first of all eat, drink, have shelter and clothing, before it can pursue politics, science, art, religion, etc.; that therefore the production of the immediate material means of subsistence and consequently the degree of economic development attained by a

given people or during a given epoch form the foundation upon which the state institutions, the legal conceptions, art, and even the ideas on religion, of the people concerned have been evolved, and in the light of which they must, therefore, be explained.[1]

The implication is that the superstructure is dependent on the base; changes in the base will eventually bring about changes in the superstructure. The central cause of any significant political transformation, for instance, must reflect changes in the economic structure. The idea is that human society is anchored to a material base the constituents of which are the productive forces and associated productive relationships. In effect, and *ultimately*, the economic structure determines the form the legal, political, moral, aesthetic, religious, philosophical characteristics of any given society will take.

In a class society, such as that engendered by capitalism, the struggle between the owning but non-working capitalist class and the working but non-owning proletariat can be resolved only through political revolution. While economics is the most crucial factor determining every relationship, political revolution is the only workable means of bringing about a change in a class exploitative society. The most desirable social condition will emerge when the state withers away and communism is instituted.

Marxism is surely teleological; it aims at transforming a given society. According to Marx, 'the philosophers have only *interpreted* the world, in various ways; the point, however, is to *change* it'.[2] This change can occur only by transforming the mode of production of material life, which alone determines the general character of other processes of life.

No doubt for Marx and Engels literary and artistic development are determined by the mode of production of material life – the economic structure which *ultimately* always asserts itself on all other activities. Nevertheless, although it is the base that determines the superstructure, the degree of interaction Marx allowed between them suggests that the superstructure can influence the development of a society. Indeed, Engels observes that 'it is not that the economic situation is cause, *solely active*, while everything else is only passive effect'.[3] A bad law or bad government can hinder production and consequently development of a society.

In a class society, where a dominant economic class ends up with determinate political and economic influence in all spheres of that society, the law is unlikely to reflect the interest of the underprivileged. Equally, given that a writer is a member of the society, he or she cannot be immune from its antagonistic class relationship. Writers can, through their work, offer critical appraisal of the existing political situation and this way can mould or redirect their society's actions, beliefs, ideals, values and ideas. In this manner ideas contained in literature can influence people's perception of politics and the best means of effecting political change.

Literature, then, should function as a reflection of the economic arrangements in society and the nature of the relationship they foster. Its purpose is to analyse society in its own terms, to present a fictional world that is a lifelike representation of the real world. Writers should approach their task as a social act that entails evaluating the mode of production in society; the nature of the relationship between the various classes; and how to bring about a revolutionary end to the oppression and exploitation by one class of another.

Writers, as members of an integral, highly complex society, are influenced by its dynamics. To this extent, literature should reflect the economic arrangement: the mode of material production; the classes and their struggles; the inevitable revolution that will sweep away capitalism and all its oppressive and exploitative devices; and the historical possibility of communism as the most desirable end product. Real change demands the recognition that transformation of society can be achieved only by overcoming the alienation of mankind from the product of its labour; reconciling knowledge with social ends; and dismantling all class structure.

Since writers live in a given environment and belong to a class, they cannot be neutral. Marxist aesthetics offers a choice for one particular artistic production over another. According to Ngugi (1981: 38), there have been two opposing aesthetics in literature, 'the aesthetic of oppression and exploitation and of acquiescence with imperialism; and that of human struggle for total liberation'. Marxist aesthetics is in agreement with the latter. It helps in the evaluation of economic relations, which ultimately plays a decisive role in the political and ideological struggles in society. Balibar and Macherey (1992: 53) observe that 'class struggle is not abolished in the literary text and the literary effects which it produces'; rather, 'they bring about the reproduction, as dominant of the ideology of the dominant class'. Marx and Engels (1968: 51), indeed, assert that the ruling ideas of each age have ever been the ideas of its ruling class.

Marxist aesthetics, then, helps to show that it is within the province of art to portray the capacity of men to struggle against all obstacles. 'From the standpoint of the revolutionary,' says Omafume Onoge

(1985a: 44), 'the political criterion of excellent art is art which serves the struggle of the people against their oppression.'

For Marx and Engels a proper understanding of aesthetics was founded on an understanding of economic relations, which *ultimately* determine the aesthetics. Where economic relation is one of gross inequality, there is need for a revolution to bring about a more humane society. The writer's task is to reflect this inequality, and advise as to how a revolution can be effected and a communist system of government installed. This is, perhaps, the crucial sense in which Marx understood aesthetics.

Ngugi: champion of Marxist aesthetics

Marx's aesthetics applies to Ngugi (1981: 96), who sees literature as 'a reflection of the material reality under which we live'. The writer's primary responsibility in Ngugi's view is to channel his or her creative energy towards the production of the aesthetic devoted to the fight for freedom, exposing the distorted values integral to the capitalist exploitative system and the struggle against exploitation in a class society. To carry out this task, a writer has to be sensitive to the class nature of the society and its influence on the imagination. Ngugi (ibid.: 71) points out that 'there is no area of our lives including the very boundaries of our imagination which is not affected by the way that society is organized, by the whole operation and machinery of power: how and by whom that power has been achieved; which class controls and maintains it; and the ends to which the power is put'.

Literature is part of the class power structures that shape our everyday life (ibid.: xii). A writer's works invariably reflect the various struggles – political, cultural, ideological, economic – going on in society. Every literature is a commitment to a particular political ideology and every writer is a writer in politics (ibid.). For literature to be meaningful it has to assume a revolutionary stance. Its focus must be on a critical appraisal of the economic structure of modern society, essential in getting a revolution going. Ngugi's ideal is for a literature that is committed, assertive and confrontational, which can bring about a more equitable change in human relations, especially in the unbalanced relationship between the West and Africa and other Third World countries. Literature is teleological; its goal must be to transform a given society.

The essential task of literature, at least for the African writer, is therefore to act as a vehicle of liberation from European imperialistic capitalism, which has placed the West at the core and Africa and the Third World at the periphery in economic and social relations. It is only a revolution that can restore to Africa and its people the positive self-image and confidence necessary for the radical transformation of society. It is the duty of the African writer to help in the struggle of building a place for African masses to feel at home (Ngugi 1972: 46). Writers must align themselves with the people, Ngugi asserts (1981: xii), to fight against 'the side of those social forces and classes that try to keep the people down'. The essence of art is to serve the struggle of the people against their exploiters. Indeed, the extent to which the writer can and will contribute not only by interpreting the world but in changing it will depend on his or her understanding of the classes and values contesting for a new order, and identifying which classes and values are obstructing the birth of the new and the hopeful (ibid.: 75).

The art-for-art's-sake notion has no place in the writing of litera-ture as far as Ngugi is concerned. He believes that it is within the possibility of the oppressed in real society to change the conditions of their lives. The Mau Mau revolt is for him a good example of the feasibility of this project. The writer's subject matter is history, the conscious acts of agents in society acting and changing nature and themselves, performing the dual role of producers and makers of history.

Literature cannot stand apart from the social processes taking place in society. Its *thoroughly social* character makes it partisan; literature takes sides, especially in a class society (ibid.: 6). For this, the African writer must shun 'abstract notions of justice and peace' and actively support the 'actual struggle of the African peoples' and in his or her writing reflect 'the struggle of the African working class and its peasant class allies for the total liberation of their labour power' which alone provides the foundation for a socialist transformation of the society (ibid.: 80). In Ngugi's summation, Marxist-oriented literature is the only literature worth producing.

Petals: a blend of vision and practice

In *Petals of Blood*, Ngugi (1977) puts this vision into practice. According to him, *Petals* is about the peasants and workers who have built Kenya (and by extension Africa), and who, through their blood and sweat, have written a history of grandeur and dignity and fearless resistance to foreign economic, political and cultural domination (Ngugi 1981: 98). Throughout the novel, Ngugi presents characters whose conduct is firmly rooted in concrete material his-tory and changing social conditions; his mission is to show that imperialist capitalism can never nurture Africa or Africans; his focus is unwavering on how to effect change in material production and class relations in Marxist terms.

Petals is a fictional account of Marx's history of class struggles: workers' organization through unions; the transformation of society through an inevitable revolution that will sweep away capitalism and all the oppressive tools it has used to enslave, divide, disunite, suppress and exploit the proletariat; and the eventual triumph of communism. Through the events that revolve round Ilmorog, the conflict in economic relations is used as the basis for portraying a revolutionary consciousness and the transformation of society.

Ilmorog, the setting of most of the novel's major social and political activities and a representation of a typical post-colonial African society, was once a thriving society with a huge population of sturdy peasants before the advent of colonialism. With colonialism came a number of changes. European farmers robbed the farmers of the virgin soil they needed for shifting cultivation. Trapped in farming and refarming their small exhausted acreage with poor implements, their production declined drastically. The youths who could have helped on the farm were lured by better facilities to work on European farms or in big towns.

The introduction of taxes by the colonial government acted as an incentive for the people to sell their labour to European farmers in order to earn the money required, which they could no longer raise through their own sterile farms. What they earn through sweated labour (which is barely enough to keep them going) they give back to the government as tax. In essence, their material condition, instead of improving, is only made worse. Instead of their earning to make it possible for them to be able to break free of their European masters, it makes them completely dependent on them. On the other hand, their old parents left at home are reduced to the barest subsistence-level farming, which equally compromises their former production status as independent producers.

Recounting his own childhood experience, Ngugi tells of how peasant Kenyans were forcibly ejected from the land they occupied and sent to another part of the country so barren that people called it the 'land of black rocks'. While blacks struggled to farm 'scruffy little strips of shamba', the white settlers owned 'sprawling green fields' which they employed the blacks to farm for 'a meagre sum of money'. Even this minimal sum ends up in the hands of the Indian trader who owns most of the shops in the area (Ngugi 1972: 48). The labouring Africans were trapped in a vicious circle of poverty, denied the benefit of the wealth of which they were the creators, and reduced to dependency relationship with the owning (but non-working) foreign capitalist exploiters. Ngugi confesses that he was horrified when, in the course of writing *Petals*, he came to realize that Kenya (and, indeed, Africa) was poor not because of anything internal, but because the wealth produced by Kenyans (and Africans) ended in developing the Western world (Ngugi 1981: 96).

Colonialism also brought with it the insidious notion that the developed countries are the highly industrialized, technologically and politically advanced ones. African societies are, by this definition, regarded as underdeveloped, backward and necessarily subordinate to the West. For them to become developed, they have to copy the West. This entails trying to adopt the Western way of life and the paraphernalia that goes with it.

Munoru, one of Ilmorog's most prosperous farmers, abandons his farm in pursuit of the Western conception of affluence. He regards his 'metal horse' as the ultimate achievement, to the utter neglect of his farm. His longing for the 'white foreigner's things' drives him to volunteer his services to carry guns and food supplies to the warring Europeans. Along with him, others also volunteered. Those who did not 'were driven into the war with the butt end of the gun' (p. 122). The war introduced them to the white man's 'metal' – money. After the war, the Africans who took part were no longer interested in their farms. Instead, they preferred to work for the Europeans so as to earn the white man's 'metal', which they in turn spent on taxes and other 'useless things of the foreigner' (p. 123). Ngugi (ibid.: 124) notes that it has always been in the interests of a robbing minority to control the minds, the consciousness, of the working majority.

In this way, developed countries are able to exercise effective power over African societies since they determine wages and also control the supply of goods. Claude Ake (1979: 112) observes that in so far as Third World countries are made to 'desire those things which the West passes off as the necessities of development and whose supply the West largely controls, they put themselves under the power of the West'. *Petals* rejects the bigoted developmental framework that ranks Western societies highest and presents the possession of character-istics of Western societies as the ideal of development. Indeed, far from explaining the problems of African societies in terms of their lack of the characteristics of Western societies, *Petals* underscores the attempt to adopt the characteristics of Western societies as the *problem* of African societies.

Events revolving round Ilmorog also point to neo-colonialism as a key factor in the decline of African societies. With independence it is expected that African leaders should focus their attention on finding what will be suitable to the African condition and its people, that they should pursue a vigorous programme of development aimed at lifting Africa from the various harmful legacies of colonialism: dependency, underdevelopment, social injustice, economic disparity, mental inferiority and distortion of culture. For Ngugi (1981: 24), neo-colonialism means the continued economic exploitation of Africa's total resources, of Africa's labour power by international monopoly capitalism through sustained creation and maintenance of subservient weak capitalistic economic structures, captained or supervised by a native ruling class.

Nderi, the MP representing Ilmorog and the quintessential representative of the African leaders who emerged after independence, differs in no way from the exploitative colonizers. He adopts their ethical code of 'greed and accumulation' (p. 163). Ensconced in the capital, he completely forgets the place he is supposed to be representing. All his attention is taken up in enriching himself and ingratiating himself with the West. He accepts offers of directorships in foreign-owned companies, and diverts the money he collects from his constituents for a water project as a security for further loans to enable him buy shares in companies, invest in land, in housing and in small business.

Next, he forms the *Kiama-kamwene* Cultural Organization (KCO) with a few friends ostensibly to 'bring unity between the rich and the poor and bring cultural harmony to all the regions' (p. 85). The poor are forced to take an oath (tea drinking) that will protect the riches of the few. The tea drinking is, of course, not free. The poor are tricked and forced to pay twelve shillings and fifty cents. And these are people 'threatened by lack of water; lack of roads; lack of hospitals' (p. 85), and whose means of sustenance is to scratch a fatigued earth. The loot collected from the 'mass tea drinking' exercise goes to make the few rich people even richer. Nderi's share runs into millions.

There are other sides to the KCO. In reality it serves to strengthen 'progressive cooperation and active economic partnership with imperialism' (p. 186). Nderi sees it as a means of creating wealthy local economic giants, as exist in the West. It is also made to act as the 'most feared instrument of selective but coercive terror in the land' (p. 186). It is employed to eliminate political opponents and suppress any resistance from the peasants and workers. Far from acting as a forum for cultural harmony, the KCO is used to ensure that nothing is allowed to narrow the economic, social and political gap between the super-rich and the super-poor. Commenting on this post-independence development, a character in *Petals* laments: 'this was the society they were building: this was the society they had been building since independence, a society in which a black few allied to other interests from Europe, would continue the colonial game of robbing others of their sweat, denying them the right to full flowers in air and sunlight' (p. 294).

By the time the Ilmorogians are forced, by severe drought, to trek to Nairobi to make their plight known to Nderi, he has become one of the richest MPs in the land. He owns 'a huge farm in the Rift Valley, a number of plots and premises in Mombasa, Malindi and Watamu, shares in several tourist resorts all along the coast' (p. 174) and many more lucrative business interests and connections. All this while the community he represents can be described as 'a deserted homestead, a forgotten village, an island of under-development which after being sucked thin and dry was itself left standing, static, a grotesque distorted image of what peasant life was and could be' (p. 184). The trek, however, makes Nderi realize the need to 'develop' the area.

Nderi, indeed, brings 'development' to Ilmorog. To start with, the trans-Africa road that links Ilmorog to many cities of the continent 'was built, not to give content and reality to the vision of a continent' (p. 262) but, rather, to pander to the recommendations of foreign experts. The road, instead of benefiting the people it is supposed to serve, ends up by exposing them to international capitalist robbery and exploitation. Lenin (1993: 174) identified transport as one area of highly developed capitalism, used by the exploiter to gain deeper access to both the natural and human resources of the colonized for the purpose of intensifying the exploitation of the people and their resources.

In exchange for their old way of life, the road creates a 'new' town out of Ilmorog and 'catapult[s]' the people into 'modern' times. Huts that stand in the way of the road are destroyed. Mwathi's, Ilmorog's guardian spirit, place is razed to the ground to make way for 'trade and progress!' This destruction obliterates the past, represented by the rings, metal work, spears and smelting works found in the place. Muturi, the location's guardian, becomes deaf and dumb at the sacrilege and dies before he can pass on the secret of Ilmorog's guardian spirit. The community loses vital knowledge.

The Chiri country council set up to plan a shopping centre at Ilmorog ends up by creating more poverty among the poor. Tillers and herdsmen are deprived of their hitherto unquestioned rights of use and cultivation of the land and are forced into 'hiring themselves out to any who needed their labour for a wage' (p. 273). Abdulla and Wanja's Theng'eta brewing licence is taken away to make way for Mzigo, Chui and Kimeria (prominent and founding fathers of KCO) to have the sole rights to brew Theng'eta. Also their bar and meat-roasting centres are closed to provide the right environment for the tourist centre owned by Nderi and a foreign partner. The Utamaduni Cultural Tourist Centre, as it is known, is ostensibly 'there to entertain Watali from USA, Japan, West Germany, and other parts of Western Europe' (p. 334). But this is only a camouflage for other more sinister activities:

> smuggling of gemstones and ivory plus animal and even human skins. It was a centre for the plunder of the country's natural and human assets. Women, young girls, were being recruited to satisfy any Watali's physical whims. The more promising ones, those who seemed to acquire an air of sophistication with a smattering of English and German, were lured to Europe as slave whores from Africa! (p. 334)

Thanks to the activities of the county council, 'every prominent person in the country owns a bit of Ilmorog: from the big factory to the shanty dwellings' (p. 282). Even the occasional clean-up, burn-down campaign undertaken by the council results in the 'shanties put up by the unemployed and the rural migrant poor razed to the ground' (p. 282), whereas similar contraptions owned by prominent landlords are not touched. Abdulla's one-room contraption of a few poles and mud is among the ten blocks owned by 'a very important person in authority' (p. 283) who charges a hundred shillings per room. The council also allocates some of the kiosks built by the trans-Africa road to some of its councillors and officials free of charge, which they then sell on for more than fifty thousand shillings to others who rent them out to female petty traders. This kind of situation makes it difficult for the petty traders to break even, let alone make a profit. So while a class appropriates the surplus without paying for it, another class toils unrewarded.

Nderi urges the people to register their lands in order to acquire title deeds, which in turn act as security with the banks without adequately explaining the consequences to them. As a result, peasants and herdsmen of old Ilmorog, who have been lured into loans and into fencing off their land and buying imported fertilizers, are unable to pay the money back and have their lands auctioned. The only option left to them is to sell their sweated labour in a market; those who are too old and powerless to do anything are left with no prospect but death, as in the case of Nyakinyua. Wanja's attempt to redeem Nyakinyua's land leads to them (she and Abdulla) selling their business building, which has taken them years to set up. Wanja turns to prostitution in order to cope with the pace of New Ilmorog, and opens the 'Sunshine lodge' – a whorehouse. She begins meticulously to plan her revenge on those – Kimeria, Mzigo, Chui – she feels are responsible for her present situation. *Petals* demonstrates the problem of spiritual and mental degradation which is an important aspect of the reality of the masses' condition under capitalism.

Abdulla's attempt to run a shop is dashed by a supermarket, which opens nearby. The competition offered by the supermarket forces him out of business and pushes him into the streets, 'almost a beggar' – and this is someone who lost a leg to the independence fight. He becomes a roadside orange seller, resolute in his ambition to kill Kimeria, who sabotaged the independence fight and is now benefiting tremendously from it.

A study (Langdon 1975) of the activities of multinational corporations (MNC) in Kenya shows how local, small, non-mechanized industries are edged out or forced to engage in wasteful change-over costs in order to stand up to the stiff competition of MNC. Lenin (1993: 170) observes that the free competition that is the basic feature of capitalism has been transformed into a monopoly, 'creating large-scale industry and forcing out small industry'. According to Ngugi (1993: 107), 'independence did not always result in the empowerment of the people. Economic power still lay in the hands of a tiny elite exercising it on behalf of the dominant interests of the West.'

In the end, Ilmorog is transformed into a 'modern' town. The New Ilmorog Shopping Centre attracts the development of wheatfields and ranches, which displace the herdsmen. Banks, a tourist centre, a brewery, churches and a whorehouse all compete in the 'scramble' and 'partition' of Ilmorog. The residential areas also mirror the different class interests. The Cape is for the rich, while 'New Jerusalem' – a shanty town of migrants and floating workers, the unemployed, prostitutes and small traders – is for the poor. This is where most former Ilmorogians end up.

So within ten years of their journey to the city, Ilmorog peasants have been displaced from their land: some join the army of workers; some became semi-workers, working both on a plot of land and in a factory; some turn to petty trading in hovels and shanties that do not belong to them along the trans-Africa road, or become criminals and prostitutes. The few who try their hands at making sufurias, karais, water tins, chicken-feeding troughs, or become shoe-makers or carpenters, are pushed out because of the stiff competition from more organized large-scale production of the same wares. In what way has Ilmorog's 'development' and 'modernization' impacted on the life of its people? How is it that the people who provided the land and the labour can barely sustain themselves? Their earlier condition and their present condition, which is better? Has 'development' for them resulted in underdevelopment? Does the Western ideology of development that is being mindlessly pursued by African leaders understand the need to distinguish between the good life and material possessions?

Claude Ake (1979: 112) points to the need not to confuse the existence of wealth and technological know-how with the good life. For him, if nations must be grouped as inferior and superior, then such classification should 'be based ultimately on the quality of life, that is, on considerations of how far a society is just, happy, free and cooperative, and how far it is free from exploitation, greed, alienation, and aggression'. Ngugi (1993: 118) questions the rationale for making black gratitude for white charity a national ideal and the expected basis of international relations between the West and African societies. What sort of 'development' will free Africa from unequal exchange, exploitation, greed and the grab-all mentality? What kind of ideology will guarantee the type of political, economic, techno-logical development that will be most suited to African conditions?

Crystallizing an ideology

The events in Ilmorog lead Karega, through whom the political ideology and artistic vision is enunciated, to probe the root cause of the problems and also to search for the solution. He tries to find answers to the following questions. Why are peasants and workers not in control of the land they fought for? What have the peasants gained from independence? How has the ruling elite tried to change the colonial social and economic structure? How is it possible that about 75 per cent of those who produce food and wealth are poor and that a small group – part of the non-producing population – is wealthy? How come parasites – lice, bedbugs and jiggers – who do no useful work, live in comfort and those who work the hardest go hungry and without clothes? Why should so few wield the power of life and death over so many? What is responsible for the building of a society in which a black few, allied to other interests from Europe, will continue the colonial game of robbing others of their sweat and sabotaging the benefit of independence? How is it that Africa, which has contributed so much to the development of the rest of the world through centuries of trade and conquest, is still referred to as underdeveloped and its people – the real producers of wealth – condemned to lead miserable lives?

Alvin Y. So (1990: 97) quotes Gunder Frank as arguing that the national transfer of economic surplus, which has its origins in the colonial period, has produced underdevelopment in Third World countries and development in Western countries. The historical process that generates development in the Western metropolises also simultaneously generates underdevelopment in Third World satellites. I. G. Shivji (1976: 17) equally maintains that the low state of development of Africa results from 'the history of the exploitation of the African people by the advanced capitalist countries'. For Claude Ake (1979: 111), 'the present condition of the third world is the effect of the slave trade, pillage, colonialism, and unequal exchange'. In *Homecoming* Ngugi (1972: 3) is categorical that 'it was African labour and Africa's material wealth that built America and the major cities of Europe'. While in *Writers in Politics* (Ngugi 1981: 11) he is emphatic that 'Europe not only underdeveloped Africa but Africa has continued to develop Europe'. Again, in *Moving the Centre* Ngugi (1993: 118) maintains that 'the wealth of the West is rooted in the poverty of the rest of us' and that (ibid.: 133) 'Europe's vaunted development is founded on Africa's underdevelopment'. So what type of system supports the plundering and concentration of a people's wealth in the hands of foreigners and a few locals who have not toiled for it, while the real producers of the wealth groan under the burden of acute poverty?

Karega discovers the root of these problems in an imperialist capitalist economy that traps people in a new kind of slavery and neo-colonialism. According to him, 'a man who has never set foot on this land can sit in a New York or London office and determine what I shall eat, read, think, do, only because he sits on a heap of billions taken from the world's poor' (p. 240). Kwame Nkrumah (1965: ix) notes that the 'essence of neo-colonialism is that the state which is subject to it while possessing outward trappings of international sovereignty is in reality dependent' for the reason that 'its economic system and thus its political policy is directed from outside'. For Ngugi (1972: 45), monopoly capitalism (and its external manifestations, imperialism, colonialism, neo-colonialism) 'whose every condition of growth is cut-throat competition, inequality, and oppression of one group by another', is what has disfigured the African past.

In *Petals* a whole family of labourers – man, wife and children – is paid one hundred shillings a month to pick sisal and tealeaves and coffee. Besides the subservient wage, the few peasants not driven off the land to make room for multinational corporations are encouraged to grow the raw material needed by the companies instead of food. The companies then buy the raw material at 'whatever price they deem fit' (p. 289). To overcome this, Karega realizes that the peasant growers need to be organized in order to protest and bargain. The whole working class needs to team up to fight oppression.

Petals champions violent revolution as a just reaction against oppression. It presents the poor condition of the masses as a weapon for triggering revolt, resistance and a cause to embark on the search for a way to end their exploitation and create a more humane world. Karega notes that the true lesson of history is that the so-called victims, the downtrodden, the masses, have always struggled with spears and arrows, with their hands and songs of courage and hope, to end their exploitation; that they will continue struggling until a human kingdom comes (p. 303). Equally, in *Writers in Politics*, Ngugi (1981: 124) observes that the robbed have always struggled for the control of the wealth they have produced, struggled against all the oppressive social institutions erected on the structure of theft and robbery.

What system, then, will end the exploitation of labour by capital? How can imperialist capitalist economy be fought and overthrown? What system will 'free the manacled spirit and energy' (Ngugi 1972: 50) of African people so they can build a new, united society? What will free African workers from economic servitude and thereby guarantee Africa's genuine political emancipation?

Karega finds the solution to the imperialist impasse in the alliance of workers and peasants to carry out a radical socialist transformation of society. For him the key to creating a 'more humane world' in which the inherited inventive genius of mankind in culture and science is put to the use of all lies with the poor, the dispossessed, the working millions and the poor peasants equipping themselves with guns, swords and organization, to change the conditions of their oppression and seize the wealth that rightly belongs to them. 'Imperialism: capitalism: landlords had to be fought consciously, consistently and resolutely by all the working people' (p. 344). 'Tomorrow it would be the workers and the peasants leading the struggle and seizing power to overturn the system of all its preying, bloodthirsty gods and gnomic angels' so as to bring 'to an end the reign of the few over the many' and 'only then would the kingdom of man and woman really begin, they, joying and loving in creative labour' (p. 344). There is a pronounced aesthetic of resistance, commitment and ultimate liberation in *Petals*.

Karega's conviction is that every dispute, every obstacle preventing African societies from achieving genuine political liberation is determined by the economic forces of production; that this is explainable in the context of the exploitation of labour by capital; that exploitation will result in the emergence of class struggle, in which the working class will inevitably overthrow their exploiters in a revolutionary combat and replace capitalism with communism. This embodies the essential features of Marxism – specifically, the revolutionary school of thought.

Marxism is a 'theory of the nature of history and politics as well as a prescription for revolutionary action to bring the industrial working class to power and create a classless society' (Daniels 1997: 388). The only workable solution to the persistent economic crisis that torments capitalist economies and the oppression of man by man that characterizes human history is worldwide socialist revolution. For Marx (Marx and Engels 1968: 51), mankind's consciousness changes with every change in the conditions of material existence; and at a certain stage in development 'the material forces of production in society come in conflict with the existing relations of production' and 'then occurs a period of social revolution. With the change of the economic foundation the entire immense superstructure is more or less rapidly transformed' (Marx 1956: 67–8).

The aim is to create a society in which huge discrepancies in power, wealth, material possessions, opportunities, privileges and, especially, private ownership of property are abolished in order to achieve justice and equality, the basis of guaranteeing cohesion, harmony and fairness in society. This is possible only in the higher phase of communist society, in which the enslaving subordination of the individual to the division of labour, along with the antithesis between mental and physical labour, will vanish; labour will cease to exist for monetary rewards but become life's principal need; and the productive forces will increase with the all-round development of the individual, and all the springs of co-operative wealth flow more abundantly. At this point, society can inscribe on its banners: 'From each according to his ability, to each according to his needs' (ibid.: 263). That is, the state has disappeared – 'withered away' – and a 'classless' communist society has been established.

Communism at its philosophical core, then, 'amounts to a belief that man could not fulfil his humanity unless society was transformed so as to liberate him from all individual acquisitiveness' (Kim 1992: 17). Without doubt, 'man could obtain true freedom only through the absolute destruction of all structures of inequality'.

Cracks on the wall: weaknesses in the inner logic of Marxist ideology

But what are the implications of identifying the Marxist revolutionary stance as the best means of resolving Africa's political impasse? The worker-peasant revolt may not be as inevitable as Karega asserts. The teleological assumption that history has a purpose that will inevitably culminate in the destruction of capitalism and the establishment of communism is not irrefutable. Marxism is premised on the economic circumstances acting as the base supporting all other institutions – whether political, legal, artistic or even military. A revolutionary attempt by the poor working class is therefore most likely to be frustrated by a circular dilemma: for the propertyless exploited workers to carry out a revolution effectively, they need to secure the economic base, and since they do not have said economic base, they cannot carry out an effective revolution. Besides, there is really no good reason to suppose that, even if capitalism has some inherent weaknesses, they are enough to lead to its disintegration. Costello (1963: 19) points out that Marx's prediction that only violence could change the injustices of capitalism failed Marx's own test of history, since capitalism has changed relatively peacefully.

Again, Karega's position implies that people think the same way on important matters, that there is a panhuman nature common to all, and that class antagonism is a given. In *Petals* Nyakinyua's attempt to organize the dispossessed of Ilmorog into a protest to fight for their land ends in some of them deriding her. The people whose lands are not to be auctioned off refuse to get involved, suggesting that, possibly, the working class will be more prepared to work within capitalism through reformist methods, rather than fight for its abolition. Jules Townshend (1996: 251) points out that 'the working class ideologically has tended towards reform rather than revolution'. Robert Daniels, equally, observes (1997: 394) that in countries (such as Britain, Scandinavia, the United States, Canada) with rising living standards and democratic access to political power, Marxism has never had more than a limited and passing appeal, and it is hard to apply the Marxian theory of proletarian revolution, however interpreted.

Given that Marxian revolution has failed to take place in highly industrialized and capitalist economies as Marx, indeed, believed, it may be equally unlikely to work in Africa. There are good grounds for such a reservation. Marx's model of two antagonistic classes does not really exist in Africa's political experience, so class politics in Africa cannot be reduced to a simple competition between bourgeoisie and proletariat (Thompson 2000: 91). For instance, in Nigeria, and indeed in most African countries, the poor standard of living of most people is such that by all reasonable criteria they should have been pushed to the brink of revolutionary violence, yet nothing of the sort has happened. Instead, poor people actively support and canvass for the rich, especially during elections. They even resort to fighting each other for the sake of their 'man'. Those who do not express themselves in this way are, often, more interested in finding ways to accommodate themselves to the hard conditions rather than channelling that energy towards a revolution they view as unprofitable.

Even supposing the poor working class in Africa embark on successful socialist revolution, it is unlikely they will sustain it once their condition changes. Far from advocating a socialist revolution, most labour unions in African societies are more interested in securing better working conditions for the workers. It appears *Petals* is mistaken about man's basic disposition. When people gain greater knowledge they may disagree on the meaning of the rules they previously adopted.

Besides, there is a problem lurking in the simple assumption that once workers become leaders all disagreement will melt away. There is an equal possibility of workers not automatically buying the ideas of their revolutionary leaders. It is also likely that extra-economic considerations – difference in national identities, religion, gender – will play an important role in shaping the economic situation. Karega discovers in the course of his wanderings that male workers denigrate the female ones; those from the same linguistic enclaves and clans and regions tend to bond; while some workers easily give up everything for their religion. In Nigeria, for instance, ethnicity and religion cause as much, if not more civil strife as economic problems.

Moreover, there is no good basis for the assumption that the worker–peasant alliance that will act as the driving force to topple the capitalist system *must* materialize. It is plausible that the different groups may end up mutually suspicious and antagonistic. Again, it is possible that exploiters will emerge among the workers. Robert Daniels (1997: 390) identifies a major weakness in the inner logic of Marxism as 'the question why the dialectic should stop once capitalism has been overthrown; why not a new ruling class exploiting the masses on some new basis?'

For a system that has taken centuries to develop, as is the case with capitalism, it may well be naïve optimism to assume that it will quickly disappear. Arthur Ripstein (1997: 287) observes that the idea of the historical inevitability of socialism was attacked for being 'unscientific, for denying the role of human choice in history, and for conceptual confusions about the relation between individual and society'. Francisco Weffort (1992: 99) is also sceptical: 'socialism, in any imaginable form, should be understood as a *possibility* rather than as a historical *necessity*'.

In addition, it is not possible to create strictly a propertyless society; even if a socialist revolution is successful, it will amount only to the transfer of private property to state ownership which, truly speaking, does not amount to the abolition of property. Instead, another kind of hegemony is established – this time at the centre. Anthony Giddens maintains (1971: 204) that in 'Marxist socialism, capital does not disappear, it is merely administered by society and not by individuals'.

It is also doubtful that the abolition of private property will really enhance human happiness. There is reason to suppose that mankind prefers a system where it is free to work and own private property. Alan Ryan (1998: 398) remarks that conservatives have argued that 'being able to look after our own portion of the world is a source of human happiness, so that private property and membership of stable communities are both valuable'. Locke considers the preservation of private property as the motive power for the emergence of civil society, and Kyung-Won Kim (1992: 18) suggests that the failure of communism is an acknowledgement that man's acquisitive drive, an inherent part of human nature, may be among the conditions necessary for a free society.

It is not plausible that those who favour capitalism will surrender easily. The success of the workers will then depend on their ability to sustain a permanent class war until the ruling class and its agents have been removed and destroyed. Given that there is no way to know beforehand the result of such a conflict, the assumption that labour must overthrow capital is at best presumptuous.

The feasibility of the new world of freedom and prosperity that will be ushered in under a communist system is also not without some difficulties. To bring about a communist system will entail a degree of serious conflict between capital and labour. Ryan rightly notes (1998: 401) that at the point where 'the "solution" to the problem of a more equitable distribution of the rewards of economic cooperation becomes the destruction of one party to the competition, politics ceases and civil war begins'. This evidently is not the kind of environment that will encourage prosperity, or even freedom. The defeat of capital will, most probably, put labour on the alert so as to suppress any insurrection. There is good reason to assert that communist societies are, indeed, more repressive than capitalist ones.

In Stalin's Soviet Union, Marxism was used to justify the oppressive, despotic methods used to maintain inequalities and the absence of many basic rights. Stalin used the notorious Moscow trials of the mid-1930s to liquidate his opponents. Prominent communists such as Aleksei Ryckov, Nikolai Bukharin, Lev Kamenev and Grigori Zinoviev were sentenced to death. Stalin made the 'fourth chapter' of the *History of the Communist Party of the Soviet Union*, supposedly written by him, compulsory reading for every literate person in the Soviet Union. And 'professional philosophers expounded it *ad infinitum*, unable to transcend its horizons for fear of challenging Stalin's authority' (Bakhurst 1998: 156). Nisbet (1982: 247) adds: 'Soviet Russia, now more than fifty years away in time from the success of the Bolshevik Revolution, is very probably the most centralized, bureaucratized and collectivized political state in history.'

Far from guaranteeing freedom, socialism closes up the social space within which individuals, groups and entire institutional complexes can develop independent of state control (Berger 1992: 12). For Jeremy Shearmur (1992: 80), there is, certainly, 'a great deal to be said for systems in which ordinary people are as much as possible left free to trust their own practical knowledge'. Kyung-won Kim (1992: 18) identifies rising citizen demands for greater freedom as a major cause of the collapse of communism across the former Soviet bloc.

In 1985, soon after assuming office, Mikhail Gorbachev introduced some reforms to encourage a new openness (glasnost) and to restructure the Soviet socio-economic order (perestroika). When Deng Xiaoping assumed power in China in 1978 he switched the economic policy from central planning to increased openness to market forces. Robert Daniels (1997: 388) reminds us that the Marxist prophecies of 'the classless society and the withering away of the state have not come true; instead the characteristic pattern of the officially Marxist societies is a bureaucratic dictatorship'. With the fall of communism in Eastern Europe, Marxism faces an even greater challenge to demonstrate its continued relevance as a political creed.

Moreover, it does not automatically follow that once someone is a worker or poor, then he or she must be exploited, and if someone is rich, then he or she is an exploiter. Karega's disagreement with the lawyer is based on the latter's refusal to agree that the only means of redeeming the system is to have a clear-cut divide between capital and labour and to put an end to private ownership of property. Although Karega sees this as a great fault, he admits that the lawyer is the 'finest and most courageous in a line of courageous and selfless individuals' (p. 301). There is no neat divide between employers and workers; there are instances where workers are also employers. Abdulla started out as Wanja's employer before they became partners. Even peasants are known to employ labour during cultivation and harvesting. It appears that Karega's narrow and strict presentation of orthodox communism cannot guarantee the broad field of culture and expression needed even for communism itself to survive.

Conclusion: not easily put out

And yet it would be a mistake to write off Karega's proposal entirely. By highlighting the shortcomings of capitalism, he demonstrates an undeniable truth: where the worker is alienated from the product of his or her labour, he or she is likely to become resentful, and this can lead to violent revolt. This situation will invariably destabilize the society as the worker views it as hostile instead of being the means of his or her self-realization.

In *Petals*, the murder of Kimeria, Mzigo and Chui, the African directors of the internationally famous Theng'eta Breweries and Enterprises Ltd, has its roots in dissatisfaction with the capitalist system and its complete disregard for moral purity. Munira's setting fire to Wanja's whorehouse (which results in the deaths) is supposed to purge society of the evils of capitalism and capitalist democracy. Abdulla and Wanja had also separately planned to kill the directors, Wanja because of the way they dispossessed her of her Theng'eta business; Abdulla because he feels the injustice of Kimeria enjoying the benefit of the independence he did not fight for, while he (Abdulla) can barely make ends meet. It is an acknowledged fact that many of the conflicts in African societies are purely economically motivated. The long-running conflict that has resulted in mass deaths in oil-producing areas of Nigeria, for instance, is based entirely on economic considerations.

Here, Ngugi seems to be pointing to two crucial considerations: the Marxist position that mankind will achieve a greater freedom if it attains a full human condition, producing without being forced by physical necessity to sell labour as a commodity; and the inherent misconception underlining the capitalist economy, that labour and remuneration are proportional.

Ngugi's approach has also contributed significantly to the analysis and understanding of African politics by showing that the dependency of African societies is partly imposed from outside the continent. Through centuries of exploitation of the resources in Africa the West has been able to entrench poverty in African societies. It is this that has turned these societies into continuous 'receivers' of the crumbs that fall from the 'master's' table. The prime obstacles to the development of African societies are the colonial heritage and the unequal international division of labour.

Given that the West needs the collaboration of African leaders to maintain this status quo, the only way to overhaul the system is through a socialist revolution that will weed out leaders whose interest are aligned to those of the West. According to Ngugi (1993: 84) there was no real change after independence because 'the African bourgeoisie that inherited the flag from the departing colonial powers was created within the cultural womb of imperialism'. Nkrumah (1965: xv) notes that the rulers of neo-colonial states derive their authority to govern, not from the will of the people, but from the support they obtain from their neo-colonialist masters. He goes further: 'the less developed world will not become developed through the goodwill or generosity of the developed powers', but rather only through 'a struggle against the external forces which have a vested interest in keeping it undeveloped' (ibid.: xix–xx). To struggle against imperialism and its comprador allies is to struggle for a truly human civilization (Ngugi 1981: 67).

Kenyan research (Langdon 1975: 12) on the activities of multinational corporations (MNC) discovered that 'MNC investment distorts industrial growth in poor areas, and confirms their dependence and underdevelopment, rather than promoting the wide-spread effects of genuine development'. Foreign interest in Nigeria's oil is the major factor drawing attention away from thriving groundnut, cocoa and other agricultural products. The result: 'Africa's leading oil producer now has the third largest number of poor people in the world' (Wallis 2002: 34). For Ngugi (1981: 96), 'no country, no people can be truly independent for as long as their economy and culture are dominated by foreigners'.

In truth, this dependency will continue unless contact with the West is kept to a minimum and reliance on foreign aid and technology stopped. Without these measures it will be difficult, if not impossible, to revamp the political economy of African societies, structured since colonialism to suit the needs of the West. A solid political economy is crucial in order for African societies to achieve genuine independence and autonomous national development. As Nkrumah points out (1965: x), 'a state in the grip of neo-colonialism is not master of its own destiny'.

In addition, by emphasizing the adverse effect of foreign domination in shaping the political terrain of African societies, Ngugi exposes the biased perspective of modernization theories. The modernization school believes that the only way African societies can achieve rapid development is to follow the Western capitalist path, preferably that of the United States (So 1990: Part One). Communism is seen as a threat to the modernization of African societies. By recognizing and pointing out another threat – imperialistic capitalism – Ngugi provides grounds for a more balanced criticism. Indeed, *Petals* makes a strong case against the inherent vices of imperialistic capitalism: the exploitation of the majority by the privileged few, the erection of money as the criterion of all values, extreme individualism, the tyranny of one class of society over another, inordinate wealth accumulation by a few at the expense of the majority.

Furthermore, by highlighting the negative impact of imperialistic capitalism, Ngugi shows why even effective democracy and human-rights programmes do not succeed in African societies. Poverty makes it easy for people to succumb to corruption and other vices, which militate against the institutionalization of democracy. Wanja prefers to become a prostitute than to 'return to the herd of victims' (p. 294), just as Abdulla is reduced to being a roadside fruit-seller. Ngugi (1993: 83) sees imperialism, both in its colonial and neo-colonial stages, as the 'one force that affects *everything* in Africa – politics, economics, culture, absolutely every aspect of human life'.

Ngugi sees (ibid.: 76–8) development as an integrated whole – covering physical survival, economic survival, political survival, cultural survival and psychological survival. The Western capitalist model foisted on African societies via colonialism cannot work for Africa, because colonialism, with its subjugative influence, was tailored to render the colonized dependent on the colonizer – politically, culturally, morally, economically, socially and physically.

Jean-Paul Sartre notes that there can be little doubt that the negative image of the colonized as inferior to the colonizer was widely accepted and that this cultural dominance created a 'dependency complex'.[4] For Claude Ake (2001: 16), the state of mind that produces subservient behaviour and attitude cannot be conducive to development. This is because 'development requires changes on a revolutionary scale; it is in every sense a heroic enterprise calling for consummate confidence'. As such it is not for people who do not know who they are and where they are coming from, for such people are 'unlikely to know where they are going'. Capitalism has also made it possible for the IMF and the World Bank to determine the lives and deaths of many in Africa courtesy of its inherent structure, which encourages unequal relationships (Ngugi 1993: 110).

For African societies to pursue meaningful development there is a need to destroy Western dominance completely. In Ngugi's conception of society as a complex in which politics, economics and culture are inextricably intertwined, capitalism cannot offer hope of progress and social justice that can be said to be accessible to all.[5] Essentially, the point for Ngugi (1986: vii) is: for African societies to achieve a fundamental social transformation, there must be a real break with imperialism, because 'imperialism and its comprador alliances in Africa can never develop the continent'.

Ngugi's sense of outrage at the disparity in wealth, power and wellbeing between owners of productive property and workers is understandable. Daniels (1997: 389) identifies the ethical appeal of Marxism (a creed of equality and fraternity) as a major factor in its political success. In *Petals*, Inspector Godfrey, although an ardent believer in the sanctity of private property, still realizes that the 'system of capitalism and capitalistic democracy needed moral purity if it was going to survive' (p. 334). The existence of socialist nations provides a challenge for capitalism and checks its activities. For Ngugi (1972: 19–20), a modern Africa can emerge only from a true national culture that 'nurtures a society based on co-operation and not ruthless exploitation, a culture that is born of a people's collective labour'.

That Marxism in its revolutionary form should appeal to Ngugi is not surprising, given Africa's experience with imperialism and capitalism and Marxism's rejection of both. Ngugi (ibid.: 45) calls attention to the fact that since capitalism, even at its most efficient, has failed to create equality and balanced human relationships in Europe and America there is no good reason to suppose that it can work in Africa.

Moreover, there is a worldwide outcry against capitalism. Joan Baxter (2002: 32) reports that the first-ever Africa social forum meeting, held in Bamako early in 2002, with participants from forty-five African countries, was directed at industrialized countries and their financial institutions, which dictate the policies that make African governments so unpopular with their people: privatization, structural adjustment, open markets and cutbacks in social services. Some of their slogans read: 'Down with the World Bank! Down with the IMF! Down with neo-liberalism! Another Africa is possible!' Baxter quotes Ahmed Ben Bella, Algeria's father of independence, who led the protesters, as declaring: 'Today in Bamako, we are burying capitalism' (ibid.). Baxter also quotes Aminata Dramane Traore as dismissing the claim of the World Bank and IMF to be leading the fight against poverty in Africa. As far as she is concerned, 'they are producing poverty. They just maintain themselves by making money from the poorest' (ibid.).

The African activists also rejected the New Economic Partnership for African Development (Nepad) developed by the Presidents of Nigeria, South Africa, Senegal and Algeria. Their claim is that this plan was developed without the participation of civil society and may well be no better than the ones imposed on Africa by the West. Chris Simpson (2002: 39) reports that 'some of Nepad's detractors argue that it does nothing to challenge the supremacy of the North and the weakness of the South'; instead, 'Nepad meekly follows the received wisdom of the IMF and the World Bank, courting the private sector and embracing globalisation at whatever cost'. To be sure, international support is required in the three fields – health, education and poverty alleviation – of special importance to Nepad. Tony Blair visited Africa – Nigeria, Ghana, Sierra Leone, Senegal – early in 2002 to support Nepad, which he calls a new partnership between Africa and the developed world.

Yet at the G8 summit in June 2002, in Kananaskis in Alberta, Canada, Nepad's representatives' hope of securing a growth rate of 7 per cent of gross domestic product with an annual US$64 billion in public and private investment, was dashed. The 'G8 Africa Action Plan' issued on 27 June 2002 instead pledged to provide additional funding to make up a US$1 billion shortfall in debt relief owned by African nations; and for each G8 country to determine its own level of aid to Africa in accordance with priorities and procedures. This, of course, is on the condition that African nations prove that they are serious about fighting corruption. Critics of Nepad have good grounds for their cynicism, especially if one compares the 'crumbs' Africa received at the summit with the sums pledged by the G8 to dismantle nuclear warheads in Russia, to cite one example.

Daniels (1997: 390) suggests that the significance of Marxism should 'be weighed as a contribution to the development of modern politics and social thought rather than as a dogma that must be condemned or taken on faith'. By studying the contemporary African political situation within a socio-economic context, Ngugi warns of the need to be wary of what is taken as development. Importantly, he provides insight on how to recognize change, what is to be regarded as progress, and a warning that the world is changeable – the exploited classes can, through a revolution, bring an end to their exploitation. Indeed, *Petals* functions as an instrument for conscientizing; it reveals how the revolutionary class stands in relation to other classes, materially and historically.

Ngugi's submissions will remain relevant so long as capitalism is unable to solve Africa's problems of neo-colonialism: dependency, underdevelopment, poverty, wars, debt crisis, ecological breakdown, global inequality, massive corruption, violence, rigging of elections, bribery, the erection of money as a standard of all values, lack of basic infrastructures, famine, water shortage and the like. Claude Ake (1992: 33) sums up: 'What socialist theory questioned was not the productivity of capitalism but its sustainability in the face of the contradictions that it engendered.'

SIX
Achebe and Ngugi on the African condition

§ The concern of Achebe and Ngugi, in *Anthills* and *Petals* respectively (and in all their works), has been with the African condition, with special focus on the political as a key determinant of the nature of other aspects of life. This common passion has, however, been manifested in two opposing tendencies in their treatment of Africa's political impasse. Achebe advocates a gradual reformist agenda, directed primarily at internal factors. Ngugi, on the other hand, calls for a clear-cut anti-imperialist consciousness, anchored in Marxist ideology, which accepts revolutionary violence as entirely justified, and socialism as the ideological guide for the resolution of Africa's problems. Underlying their different visions are differences in their overall assessment of some key issues: the value of class analysis; the place of dependency in Africa's underdevelopment and the role of leadership in social change.

Class analysis

Ngugi Ngugi views class conflicts (the antagonism between capital and labour), as a key factor in understanding contemporary African politics. The exploitation of labour that characterizes a capitalist economy is possible only if workers are unaware of their strength and/ or lack the willingness to utilize it. By using class as the key defining feature of society, Ngugi portrays the value of conscientizing workers and helping them recognize their strength and power. Owners of the means of production cannot by themselves produce anything; they need the workers to be able to engage in the productive process.

The workers can, therefore, decide whether to allow themselves to be perpetually exploited. According to Marx 'the history of all hitherto existing society is the history of class struggles'.[1] The social order in primitive society, due to its egalitarian character, was devoid of class distinctions. With increase in production and the establishment of private property, society was pitted into two classes, the rich (the exploiters) and the poor (the exploited). The attempt by the rich to consolidate and maintain their position and the effort by the poor to break out of their subordinate position became the source of class struggle. Since the proletarians 'have a world to win' and 'have nothing to lose but their chains' (Marx and Engels 1968: 63), they believe that 'their ends can be attained only by the forcible overthrow of all existing social conditions'.

The realization of this in *Petals* prompts the workers to unite in order to stop their exploitation. Karega's arrest and incarceration by the government to prevent the workers' revolt suggests the fear of those in authority that once the workers decide to utilize their strength and power, a new balance of class forces will emerge. It also reveals how the inequality created by exploitation by owners of production is transferred to state level.

Class analysis is particularly important in determining the relationship between African states and civil society. The Marxist theory of the state conceives the state as a product of class division.

The acquisition of private property creates the need for an institution to protect the property of private individuals against the communistic traditions of common ownership; to place the seal of general public recognition on new forms of acquiring property; to perpetuate the right of the property-owners to exploit the non-possessing classes and the rule of the possessing class over the propertyless class. The state, according to Engels, was invented for these reasons.[2]

Unlike the communal society organized by kinship, the state is organized territorially, and is more complex than primitive society and more expensive to maintain; taxes are necessary. An elaborate public force is also needed to oversee the affairs of state and to keep in check the antagonism of the two classes. Although the state should be an arbiter of class conflict and be independent from all elements of society, it usually functions as an instrument of the ruling, economically dominant class for the suppression of the exploited class. Marx and Engels (1968: 37) summed up this view in the 'Communist Manifesto': 'the executive of the modern state is but a committee for managing the common affairs of the whole bourgeoisie'.

The implication is that the state exists for the protection of the interests of the ruling class and as an instrument of class domination: 'political power, properly so called, is merely the organised power of one class for oppressing another' (ibid.: 53). For instance, in antiquity, slave owners ensured that the laws formulated and enforced were favourable to them; in feudal society landowners protected their interests via the law; and in capitalist society, as we have it today, the bourgeoisie uses the law as a weapon against the proletariat.

The state is, then, not class-indifferent. The existence of opposed interests means that the state rules to the economic advantage of the bourgeoisie and the economic disadvantage of the working class. To ensure that the working class is subdued and kept from rebelling against those whose position it favours, the state employs force and perpetuates an ideology that represents the worldview and interests of the dominant class. For the Marxists, armies, police, officials, judges, courts, punishment and prisons make up the state. Lenin (1965: 10) puts it this way, 'it [the state] consists of special bodies of armed men who have at their disposal prisons, etc.'. The state is an organization that 'within a given territory, makes and upholds by force and threat of force the rules of conduct that foster the interests of a ruling class' (Acton 1972: 237). The authority of the state derives not from free consent but from fear of coercion.

For Marxists, it is an illusion to suppose that the state exists as a unifying factor, for harmonizing the class differences of civil society. Instead, by helping the ruling class protect and maintain its position, the state acts as an instrument for alienating the poor in society. The state is an expression of the mode of production. The owners of the means of production are provided with an environment conducive to the exploitation of non-owners. Capitalists have the right to surplus value realized through the sweat of their workers.

The primary function of the state is 'the organization of the ruling class for the protection of its fundamental interests, and, above all, the form of property which this class represents' (Konstantinov et al. 1982: 295). Indeed, 'the state is only a transitional institution which is used in the struggle, in the revolution, to hold down one's adversaries by force; it is pure nonsense to talk of a free people's state'.[3] The state is a temporary phenomenon, and there is nothing like the 'free' people's state. Laws and state policies exist to serve the interests of the ruling class. The law, instead of acting as a tool for establishing and ensuring equity, obscures power relationships. For instance, workers have the right to sell labour (even if they are paid a sub-human wage) and capitalists have the right to pocket surplus value. The state is in 'contradiction' to the real interests of all members of society, constituting 'an illusory community serving as a screen for the real struggles waged by classes against each other' (Mclellan 1980: 209).

The consolation is that the state, being a temporary phenomenon, will eventually wither away. The antagonism between capital and labour will lead eventually to the overthrow of capital by labour. By utilizing their numerical strength and position as the real producers of wealth, the proletariat will be able to abolish capital through a revolution. To transform society from a capitalist to a communist one will require 'a political transition period in which the state can be nothing but the revolutionary dictatorship of the proletariat'.[4]

With the abolition of private property and the interest of the proletariat in establishing an equitable classless society, the state loses its attribute as a specific form of class domination. With the withering away of the state, true democracy is established. It is only at this point that labourers are no longer alienated from their work, production is organized 'on the basis of a free and equal association of the producers' and society will be able to inscribe on its banners 'from each according to his ability, to each according to his needs' (Marx 1956: 263).

The role of the state in post-colonial Africa is very much the same as the Marxist conception of the state. To begin with, colonialism introduced a new political order into African societies by establishing territories and boundaries where none had hitherto existed. Africans of different ethnicity, culture, religion and language were brought together to form a state. This was done for the administrative and exploitative convenience of the colonizers. Given the numeric disadvantage of the colonizers when compared with the host community, force had to be employed to collect taxes and to maintain power and authority; the state was used as a coercive instrument to exert compliance, serving as a weapon for the few members of the ruling class, while alienating the colonized. Indeed, the state was made up of armies, police, officials, judges, courts, punishment and prisons, put in place to force the colonized into submission.

It was the administrative officers who determined the kind of development desirable for the state. Given that the colonizers' motive was self-interest, even facilities such as hospitals, dispensaries, pipe-borne water, and electricity were set up to ensure the health of the European administration and primarily for their exclusive use. The construction of roads, railways and harbours (using Africans as free or grossly underpaid labourers) was principally undertaken to facilitate the movement of goods and raw materials to and from colonizing countries. There was no attempt made to encourage manufacturing and industrialization.

Instead, African countries were encouraged or forced to produce raw materials, such as groundnuts, rubber, cocoa and cotton for the colonizers' home industries. And, naturally, the expatriate firms and companies were the ones to fix the prices at which they would buy these raw materials. Also, in African countries where mineral resources were available, the exploitation was exclusively left to expatriate firms. In this way the colonial powers were able to exert complete control over Africans. Even the schools set up to educate Africans were designed principally to provide the modicum of education considered necessary to produce Africans suitable to assist the colonizers.

Eventually, it was to this class that the colonizers handed over power. In post-colonial Africa those who emerged as leaders are made up for the most part of petit-bourgeois nationalists more concerned with replacing Europeans in the leading positions of power and privilege than with effecting a radical transformation of the state and the society around it (Nzongola-Ntalaja 1987: 73). So although African states are 'independent', the colonial structure is perpetuated. In *Petals* Karega is remanded in prison because he is suspected of being a communist at heart (Ngugi 1977: 344). The leaders still maintain their distance from, and superiority over, the ruled and still utilize the state as an instrument for self-aggrandisement, intimidation and oppression. The ruled, on their part, still view the state as an alien institution that must be subverted. Claude Ake's observation (2001: 6) is apt:

> At independence the form and function of the state in Africa did not change much for most countries in Africa. State power remained essentially the same: immense, arbitrary, often violent, always threatening ... Politics remained a zero-sum game; power was sought by all means and maintained by all means. Colonial rule left most of Africa a legacy of intense and lawless political competition amidst an ideological void and a rising tide of disenchantment with the expectation of a better life.

The post-colonial state is, equally, not class-neutral. It functions as the instrument of class domination. Those who control state power use it to make policies that help to consolidate their domination, politically and economically. The subordinate social class has to struggle against its disadvantaged position in order to better its lot. The independence the state ought to enjoy from the social classes and its aspirations towards harmonizing the discordant elements of civil society are heavily compromised. The state does not in any way correspond to the liberal notion of it as a public force which is objective in the sense that it is public and which uses its monopoly of coercion to protect individual rights and liberties.

The state is, rather, the source of both power and wealth in Africa. Given this situation, the competition to control it is often intense to the point of draining and subverting the state itself. Christopher Clapham (1985: 40) observes that in a situation where the state provides a source of power and wealth that is completely disproportionate to that available from any other organized force within society, 'the quest for state power takes on a pathological dimension'. Instead of serving as an agency for extraction and control, the state acts as a prize in a political competition, and as a means by which the winners can serve their ambitions and suppress their opponents (ibid.: 41).

In *Petals*, class exploitation is entrenched and maintained within state structures. Nderi, the MP for Ilmorog, uses his control of state power to accumulate wealth, to invest in commercial projects, to dispossess the poor of their lands and allocate them to himself and his friends, to imprison innocent citizens, and to intimidate his political opponents, some to the point of murder. Access to political power is as important as or equivalent to ownership of the economic means of production. The hegemonic character of the state fails completely to cater for the welfare of the masses. *Petals* concludes that there is need for a structural transformation of the state so as to decentralize state power to prevent its abuse.

Through class analysis, Ngugi also highlights the need for power-sharing arrangements to be put in place. By focusing on the problems of people whose interests are under-represented or completely ignored, *Petals* attempts to offer a way out of the inequality of African societies. The practice whereby those who own the means of production can easily satisfy their material wants and secure political power for themselves, while those who have only their labour power to sell are reduced to a subhuman existence, alienates the masses and de-civilizes society. For the masses to feel a sense of belonging to the state, their interests must be protected by the state. This can come about, at least according to *Petals*, only by the workers, the peasantry and other disadvantaged groups asserting their claims to state resources through a violent takeover.

The need to show concern for others' wellbeing and to shun the inordinate pursuit of self-interest is represented in Ngugi's class analysis. Karega identifies the evils of an unregulated market economy in the overemphasis on the self-first, individual competitiveness, grab-all mentality, the commodification of labour. To counter this, he sees the workers' and peasants' revolt as a required condition whereby civil society might enforce a new ethos in which equity, justice, fairness, transparency, accountability and common respect for the dignity of all life are made the codes of public conduct and the basis for social, economic and political relations. Karega is convinced that the communal ethos – fraternity, co-operation for common ends – is the sustaining force of African societies. It is not surprising, then, that almost every African head of state professes to have at least some concern about guaranteeing social justice and human dignity.

Moreover, by employing class analysis Ngugi helps simplify Africa's complex political reality. This can equally be seen as a weakness; indeed some scholars (Thompson 2000; Chabal and Daloz 1999; Turok 1987) are of the opinion that class politics in Africa defies a reduction into a simple competition between capital and labour, the exploiter and the exploited. But the point is that the nature of Africa's political reality is so complex as to frustrate any attempt to build a conceptual framework for it. And yet it is important to study and understand reality as far as it can be understood. It is therefore important to formulate models to help in both conceptualizing and advancing the understanding of reality. To the extent, even if limited, that Ngugi's Marxist ideology has helped in providing an insight into African politics, its value must be acknowledged. More importantly, it provides greater epistemological space and freedom for the study of the political condition of the minorities and other disadvantaged and marginalized groups.

Besides, class analysis can be used to enhance understanding of the relationship between the developed world and African developing economies. *Petals* is explicit in its condemnation of what imperialist capital is doing to the economy and political stability of African societies. Karega condemns unequal imperialist trade arrangements as responsible for the crisis in African societies. Such condemnatory criticism may have contributed to the body of literature that has helped sensitize people to the problem of economic and political inequality that exists between developed and African countries. Ngugi's position helps direct attention to the need to address this unequal imperialist trade and its facilitative and political arrangements.

But perhaps what Ngugi wants to emphasize most, through his class analysis, is that government in a capitalist society, because of its class structure, can never guarantee security of person and promote equal justice between individuals. The reason is clear: the nature of opportunities, the avenues for taking part in decision-making, work, residence, health, education, recreation and even life-span, are determined according to a person's position in the class structure.

Many incidents in *Petals* highlight this position. The poor and powerless are forced to pay to take an oath that will ensure the safety of a few rich people and their property – property that is, in fact, stolen from the poor. Nderi easily diverts the money meant for community development to a personal fund. Abdulla and Wanja are thrown into the street and their business taken over by prominent capitalists, Mzigo, Chui and Kimeria. A whole family's labour for a month is worth only one hundred shillings, while the employers (who do not produce anything) live in flagrant opulence. The peasants of llmorog are rendered homeless and landless to make way for the capitalists. The poor are placed in a position where they have to act perpetually as factory workers or farmhands, doing routine, dull and often unrewarding tasks; exposed to dangerous conditions, often without any social security package, while another group acts continuously as a ruling class both economically and politically.

These instances point to the difficulty of guaranteeing security of person, equality or even liberty as long as this exploitation continues. For instance, it will be difficult to achieve equality in the face of the severe restriction on the scope of many people's choices in economic, political and social life. In the face of massive economic, social and political inequalities it may be impossible for human beings to realize their full or even average potential. Ngugi sees no better means of exposing these iniquities and bringing about a new order than through class analysis.

Achebe Achebe (1987: 99) sees the matter differently: through Ikem in *Anthills*, he suggests that the argument for violent revolution overlooks man's disposition to surprise. Mankind may react in a completely opposite manner from what is expected of it. The workers and the poor masses may decide to accommodate themselves to the hard realities of life instead of carrying out a revolution. This is, in fact, the case in most African countries. The poor standard of living of most people in African societies is such that they should have been pushed to the brink of revolutionary violence, yet nothing of the sort has happened. Instead, the masses usually devise new ways of reconciling themselves to their disappointment. This 'free spirit', this puzzling aspect of human nature, is what Ikem in *Anthills* (ibid.) insists that 'no system can change'.

Achebe equally questions the rationality of reducing political reality to a series of binary opposites: ruling class and masses; exploiter and exploited, employer and employee; oppressor and oppressed, capital and labour. For him, such a reduction will not help in identifying enduring solutions to Africa's political crisis. Such stratifications are flexible and susceptible to alteration, especially in Africa where class formation is still malleable. *Anthills* (ibid.: 158–9) shows that employee and oppressor can easily co-exist in one person, as shown in the attitude of civil servants who sabotage the development of the nation by their shiftlessness and fraud.

Achebe's point is that poverty or being oppressed does not make a saint of a man. The masses taking over power is not a sufficient, or even a necessary condition to guarantee good governance. Among the poor, the oppressed, there will be 'new oppressors readying themselves secretly' (ibid.: 99) even before the revolution has started. Rather than expend useful energy on class war, attention should be directed towards creating a society where people can freely realize their potential and perform their duties and obligations. Adopting a bipolar mentality is most likely to endanger and frustrate this realization.

Achebe is also opposed to Ngugi's idea that a revolution necessarily has to be violent before a new order can be established. Violence is not a compulsory precursor to bringing about a new order or to a collapse of an old one. What is needed is meaningful action, a non-violent revolution that gradually transforms society in an enduring way. Achebe's concern is that, although a violent revolution may succeed in dismantling the old order, it may not possess a lasting structure to put in its place – 'the rising, conquering tide, yes; but the millennium afterwards, no!' (ibid.). And yet to preserve the new order is vitally important. To prevent this kind of impasse, African societies are better off adopting 'piece-meal, slow and undramatic' (ibid.) approaches towards reordering their societies.

Besides, what is the point of advocating a classless society? Achebe sees such a society as a breeding ground for all the atrocities – authoritarian politics, new oppressors, centralized dictators, repression of individual freedom, lack of creativity – it is meant to eliminate. For a society to thrive and progress, there is need for differences in interest, ideology and even class. It is this variety that provides a legitimate basis for dispute. Ikem points out (ibid.: 100) that 'contradictions if well understood and managed can spark off the fires of invention'.

Moreover, African revolution does not stand a chance against world imperialism, as Ngugi seems to think. There is no way to bring about such a revolution on a global scale, since this is the only possible measure of confronting world imperialism. Ikem reminds us (ibid.: 99) that 'there is no universal conglomerate of the oppressed'. Given the impossibility of setting up such a fraternity – due to the existence of different camps of the oppressed, conflicting nationalities, interests, political ideologies and even economic backgrounds – such an eventuality is almost inconceivable.

The summation of Achebe's position is that 'orthodoxy whether of the right or the left' (ibid.: 100) cannot offer the solution to Africa's political problems. What is needed is a persistent, stubborn, consistent and gradual reformist agenda – a 'new radicalism', 'clear-eyed' enough to identify Africa's problems correctly and address them directly.

Dependency in Africa's underdevelopment

Ngugi Achebe and Ngugi also differ in the interpretations they give to Africa's problems of dependency and underdevelopment. Ngugi sees these as a reflection of the structurally unequal manner in which Africa was bought into the global economy. He believes that Africa's systematic impoverishment is an inevitable consequence of colonialism and the effect of European capitalist imperialism. Africa's progress has been, and continues to be, hindered because of the exploitation of the West.

The colonialist interest in Africa was purely in exploiting the continent and its resources. Africans were turned into producers of primary crops required for export. They did not determine even the price at which these products were to be sold. And to make sure that Africans did (still do) not engage in manufacturing, European goods were (still are) imported and multinational corporations set up to destroy local manufactures, crafts and industries. This policy ensured (still ensures) that Africans were (are) perpetually at the mercy of industrialized countries. Without control of the mainsprings of the economy – the means of production, distribution and exchange – African leaders could not (still cannot) challenge the aggressive policies of the rich industrialized countries. Zwingina notes (1972: 43) that 'the neocolonial direction of the economy was a deliberate policy of the colonial regime, which prevented Africans from economic participation'. In *Petals*, Africans are encouraged to spend their meagre income, earned from working for the colonialists, on 'useless things of the foreigners' (Ngugi 1977: 123); and those who attempt to set up local industries are forced out of the market because of the stiff competition offered by multinational corporations.

This trend has continued till today. Existing international economic relations are still biased against African countries. The place of Africa's economies in the world trade system is still largely that of primary production undertaken by farmers who cannot exercise effective price control. Political leaders who could have worked towards a change are compromised by directorship offers in foreign-owned companies. Nderi is a good example of post-independence African leaders.

To address this situation, there is a need to discontinue economic relations with the former colonial powers, to erase capitalism from African economies, and to hand over the control and resources of the state to the workers and the peasants – the actual producers. It is the active and full participation of the people in taking charge of their wellbeing that will bring about the needed transformation in terms of equitable distribution. The gap between policy and implementation – which seriously impedes political progress in Africa – will narrow because as the makers of the policy, the people will ensure its implementation. Ngugi sees this human-centred approach – the empowerment of the masses through a revolution – as a sure way of guaranteeing meaningful development and checking the legacy of dependency.

Achebe Achebe offers a different insight into the problem of dependency and underdevelopment in Africa. For Achebe (1987: 158), rather than 'heap all our problems on the doorstep of capitalism and imperialism', attention should be refocused on internal stock-taking. The attitude of corrupt and incompetent African governments is crucial in perpetuating the political environment where it is impossible to achieve any form of development. Leaders, such as Sam in *Anthills*, get into public office without preparation or any foreknowledge of what governance entails. This makes it impossible for them to formulate practicable policies or to attempt any structural transformation. To cover up their inability and unwillingness to tackle these problems, they pander to the West, while blaming it for whatever is going wrong in Africa. Achebe sees this unwillingness to accept and assume responsibility for internal shortcomings as a key factor keeping Africa dependent and underdeveloped, a result not of helplessness but, rather, the unwillingness of leaders to accept their responsibilities and act as role models.

Added to this is the activity of some members of civil society who are in a position to know better: civil servants and students, who through negative conduct work against the development of their countries. In *Anthills*, the activities of workers and students are portrayed as anti-development; instead of using their position to work for the progress of the nation, they use it as a weapon of sabotage and exploitation. They loot the public treasury, destroy public facilities or render them non-functional, engage in electoral merchandising, and make it impossible for those in rural villages to benefit from modern life (ibid.: 157–60).

For Achebe, to view dependency and underdevelopment as purely externally induced fails to reflect the internal complex and paradoxical realities of Africa. The exclusive focus on the unequal relationship between African societies and developed countries and the reliance on violent revolution as the only means of effecting change can only hinder the search for better guidelines for action. Political phenomena are not so rigidly polarized. The fluid nature of politics is an important consideration in advancing understanding of the intricacies of Africa's present political predicament. Ultimately, what is needed are committed leaders who can bring about a positive change in general social attitudes, formulate good and workable public policies, set priorities and abide by them.

Leadership in social change

Ngugi The last point to be considered as an underlying reason for Achebe's and Ngugi's different ideological perspectives is the divergence of their views on the role of leadership in social change. For Ngugi, the issue of state management is essentially the question of who should control resources – the producers or the owners of capital? The situation whereby non-producers who live off the productive activity of others in sumptuous luxury are the ones controlling state affairs, while the producers groan under the burden of abject poverty and are denied access to state power, is seen as the central cause of political crisis.

Political office-holders, such as Nderi, under a capitalist regime use their position to entrench structures of domination which enable them to convert their offices into 'looting' centres at the expense of the welfare of the people. This creates a wide margin between power-holders and the people, which works against the achievement of economic prosperity, self-fulfilment, social development and political stability. To create a humane society for a stable political order to emerge and be sustained, there is need for a decentralization of power and a more equitable distribution of resources, wealth and privileges. This condition can be brought about only by the people utilizing their strength as the real producers of state wealth and resources to overthrow the leaders and establish, in Karega's words, 'the Kingdom of man and woman ... joying and loving in creative labour' (Ngugi 1977: 344).

This, however, does not give a clear picture of how Ngugi conceives the future after the revolution. There is no well-grounded presentation of how political power should be organized, after the capitalist relations of production have been abolished; how new leadership should be constituted; the procedure of removing this leadership from office; and how unworkable policies can be changed or modified.

Ngugi does not go beyond the joy the earth will experience when the workers and their allies take over the affairs of government. This may imply that those involved in the struggle should play an equal part in defining the future. It is, however, difficult to see how this can be achieved without any guidelines, some rules set down by some authority. It is problematic to imagine how the handing over of state control to the masses might be all that is needed to transform economic, social and political relations. But perhaps it is too much to expect that a work of fiction can cover these assignments. What is important is the train of thought towards finding a way to resolve Africa's problems that Ngugi's ideology has set in motion.

Achebe Achebe presents the issue from a different perspective. For him, to transform African societies what is needed is not one class overthrowing the other, but good leadership whereby leaders can act as role models. It is these leaders who should create a new order that will ensure that the interests of minorities and other disadvantaged and peripheral groups are protected. Ikem points to the failure of rulers to 're-establish vital inner links with the poor and dispossessed' as responsible for the multiple problems that African societies are experiencing (Achebe 1987: 141).

Achebe's point is that a system cannot make itself work, nor is it plausible to expect a disciplined citizenry to exist in a society where there is no good leadership. The issue, then, is not a transfer of power to the proletariat, but the recruitment of competent leaders who understand the art of governance and who can achieve development and hence promote the general public welfare.

SEVEN
Which way for Africa?

Which way, then, for Africa? A Marxist ideology: a move towards structural transformation by empowering the people to take over the reins of government through a violent revolution and the establishment of a classless, humane, communist society? Or a reformist, leader-centric agenda – a 'new radicalism' that welcomes different ideas and aims at piecemeal, consistent, gradual transformation of society? Which of the ideologies – Achebe's or Ngugi's – will better promote trust and restore confidence to the cynical and shaken societies of Africa in the twenty-first century? Which will better bring about effective political rule, economic survival and the redressing of social inequities, ethnic differences and religious conflicts facing African societies today?

The solution may not lie in adopting any of the proposals as an isolated variable. Aggregate acceptance of any of the ideology will obscure important differences across the continent. There is no need for homogeneity of political ideology among all African states. What is called for is an ideology or ideologies that will best promote the accomplishment of acceptable political goals with minimum political stress for a given African country. What may work best for one particular state may not be appropriate for another. Even what works for a particular state at one time may not work at another.

The analytical approach should, therefore, be kept open to allow for necessary subtractions, additions, remodifications and even divisions. What may be needed in Achebe's and Ngugi's case is a higher synthesis that will transcend and harmonize the essentials of their divergent views and go beyond them to incorporate what both may have missed.

The point of recognizing the inadequacies of Achebe's and Ngugi's positions is to reconcile them in a way that presents the best course of social reconstruction for Africa to follow. The basic question of social co-ordination in Africa is how to build a society where people can freely realize their potential and perform their duties and obligations. To achieve this, there is a need to examine the process, institutions and agency that make up our political life.

Process

The issue of process has to do with how to entrench democracy. The essence of democracy is to create a society where all members are to be considered politically equal. Robert Dahl identifies five aspects of the democratic process essential for ensuring the political equality of members in a society. These are effective participation; voting equality; enlightened understanding; control of the agenda and inclusion of adults.[1] Ngugi's position is that democratic government is absolutely unrealizable in a capitalist society. The constraints (chiefly exploitation, accumulation, inequality and polarization) imposed by the capitalist relations of production make the entrenchment of the democratic regulation of life an impossibility. The only way democratic politics can root itself and be sustained is for society to be transformed. This entails an examination of the role of the state and, especially, the way it engenders class division. Marx, indeed, maintained that true democracy could come about only after the withering away of the state. This is because the role the state plays in protecting and maintaining the interest of the property class against non-property-owners prevents the emergence of a society composed of a free and equal association of producers.

The state in a capitalist society is highly compromised because of its dependence on the owners of production. The material resources by which the state apparatus survives are controlled by the owners of production. To ensure its own stability, the state has to formulate policies favourable to the objectives of the economically dominant class. This implies that the state directly serves the interests of property-owners. The state, then, is a 'superstructure' of which the 'foundations' are economic and social relations. Given that it is economics that *ultimately* determines state policies, it is impossible for there to be 'equal justice' or 'political equality' between individuals. Moreover, there is no way to bring about liberty while the state helps to entrench and support human exploitation. Freedom can come about only when people are treated equally, necessitating an association 'in which the free development of each is the condition for the free development of all'.[2]

For Ngugi social relations in African society today, which is characterized by the co-existence of extreme poverty and affluence, cannot be resolved by token gestures to democracy. The idea that presents people and their circumstances as the same hides the true condition of society. It is difficult, if not impossible, for a person in the grip of poverty to aspire to a political office or meaningfully to exercise a voting right. Equally, the law is expected to protect the interests of the people in society. Yet the law in a given society is a 'superstructure', which develops on the foundation of economic and social relations. In a class society, where a dominant economic class ends up with determinate political and economic influence in all spheres of that society, it is important to understand that the law does not reflect the interests of the underprivileged.

In *Petals* the law is readily evoked as the basis for auctioning off the land of the poor people in Ilmorog. Abdulla's and Wanja's licence to manufacture Theng'eta is taken away from them under the guise of the law and the sole right granted to the three prominent capitalists, Mzigo, Chui and Kimeria. The point is that a judge or a law enforcement officer who has no interest in politics and is interested in ensuring justice will still serve the interest of the ruling class so long as the law is not sufficiently sensitive to class interest. The only way to sustain security of person and property and to uphold equal justice is to conquer and smash the biased structure of the state.

Achebe shuns this overemphasis on the class character of society and the dismantling of the state as the means of bringing about true democracy. He considers other factors, such as ethnicity or religious differences, as equally vital in entrenching injustice in society. Excessive focus on class division offers a limited vision of the African predicament. What is needed is a more comprehensive understanding of the state – how the activities of both the propertied and non-propertied classes are responsible for the creation of class formation and consolidation, perpetuation of life leaders, state domination, excessive acquisition, untamed corruption – rather than the restricted notion that state functionaries always and deliberately serve the interests of the economically dominant class to which they belong.

Besides, Achebe does not consider capitalism as essentially anti-democratic. If anything, it provides social space for individuals, groups and institutions freely to pursue their interest independent of state control. Achebe considers individuals' freedom of choice, healthy competition with one another, the state as an institution for the protection of 'life, liberty and property' and the provider of the right environment for the pursuit of private initiatives and public concerns as essentials of democracy. He does not see how the withering away of the state or the handing over of power to the dictatorship of the proletariat can engender democracy. In *Anthills*, Ikem dismisses the idea of the necessity of putting the nation under the 'democratic dictatorship of the proletariat' (Achebe 1987: 115). Rather than result in desirable democratic consequences, Ikem points out that it will foster anti-democratic attitudes: tyranny, authoritarian politics, centralized dictatorships, new oppressors and the suppression of individual freedom, resulting in a graveyard of creativity.

Whatever the differences between Achebe's and Ngugi's positions may be, one thing is clear: entrenching democracy is necessary. To achieve true democracy will require the complete transformation of state and society. There is a need, as Ngugi insists, to revolutionize the state structure inherited from colonialism. To do this, it is vital that a precise diagnosis of the class character of African society, as Ngugi proposes, is taken into consideration in working out a programme for the transformation of African states. Equally crucial is the transformation of society: bringing harmony instead of social divisions based on ethnicity, class, religion, gender, education and other such considerations; and bringing alienated members of the society into the state fold. There is a need for a programme of (re)orientation and (re)-enlightenment to help the people understand the social forces affecting their lives (given the devastating legacy of colonialism); and a well-articulated social policy to improve people's wellbeing, to guarantee them rights to employment, to education, to health, to relief from poverty and to pursue their creative endeavours.

To conclude, a note of caution should be sounded. Since to entrench true democracy in Africa will require complete structural and societal transformation, it is important to emphasize that this will be a gradual, time-consuming process. Tolerance, consistency and patience will be necessary. Given that there are many differences between Africa's fifty-four states, the process of democratization for each must necessarily vary. Each country must work out its own realistic timetable.

It is equally important to note that entrenching democracy may not completely guarantee the good life for all the people of Africa. Whatever system of government is in place, some people will always be dissatisfied, unhappy and even treated unjustly. The greatest advantage of democracy is that, through it, some of the major problems in Africa (and, indeed, in any human society) stand a chance of being resolved.

Institutions

The issue of how to guarantee that different organs of government – institutions – protect the interests of the people is also crucial in the search for ways to resolve African problems. Ngugi, indeed, considers this issue decisive. Liberation from colonial rule resulted only in African leaders taking over the institutions of the colonial state rather than transforming them. Given the exploitative structure of the colonial state, the different organs of government protect only the interests of the economically dominant class.

For Ngugi the only way to protect the interests of exploited members of society is to institute a central economy. This is vital in helping to expose the conditions of imperfect competition that underlie a free market economy. Under such an economy it is possible for those who work, who generate surplus, to have nothing to show for it because of the inherent flaw in such a market system, whereas those who produce nothing may be the ones to live off the productive activity of others because of their access to power or their control of the means of production. In *Petals*, Nderi's position as the MP of Ilmorog is all he needs to become one of the wealthiest men in Kenya. On the other hand, all that Abdulla's hard work and ingenuity can gain for him is his reduction to a street orange-hawker.

In a 'free' market economy a narrow class of government officials and their friends or business associates can misdirect the flow of capital and resources, enrich themselves at the expense of the people with few or no consequences, as events in Ilmorog amply illustrate. The freedom taken for granted as an index of a free market economy may be illusory. People's interest is served and protected according to their position in society. Breaking out of the bondage of poverty has little or nothing to do with effort or the numbers of labour hours invested. The conception underlining the free market economy, that labour and remuneration are proportional, is a sham. What counts is capital. Societal transformation cannot be achieved because different organs of government – the executive, the legislature, the judiciary and even the military and police – are tied to capital.

Achebe paid scant attention to the issue of government institutions. Still, his objection to a centralized economy as a way of protecting the interests of the people against the different organs of government is clear. He sees such a move as likely to inhibit the creative instincts of individuals. Having a defined pattern, method, model, strategy of pursuing economic interest, as favoured under a centralized economy, is bound to bring disastrous consequences for the overall progress of society. In a situation where people must work within a set pattern, limit and remuneration, interest and opportunities for new adventures and inventions will be stifled, or even killed. Even if the economy is booming and people's comfort satisfied it will, still, be at a great cost to their freedom for self-expression. Besides, it cannot be taken for granted that people must prefer economic comfort if its price is to deprive them of the opportunity to put their creativity to use, especially since there is a chance of their equally attaining economic comfort under a free market economy.

All the same, it is important to set institutional limits that will make it possible for people who actually toil to produce the wealth to be adequately remunerated. This can be achieved through institutionalized accountability, reasonable wages, and the provision of welfare – houses for the homeless, creation of new jobs, free education, medical care, good and affordable transport – that will greatly ameliorate the living conditions of the people. If the producers are not adequately cared for and are allowed to go hungry, unsheltered and poorly clothed, it will affect their productivity and turn them into a liability for society.

This should not, however, prevent private choices, nor should it curb the expression of individual creativity. Not to allow for differences in choice would be to assume that there is a complete agreement on value and, possibly, on belief. The aim is to put in place institutional checks that will protect people's welfare and at the same time provide enough space for private expression to be conceived, realized and nurtured. There is, therefore, a need for policies that will provide a balance for private choices and public interest to be served and protected as well as to guarantee steady economic growth.

Agency

Finally, the issue of how to guarantee that those who rule are accountable to the people is also an important consideration in seeking for means of reordering African societies. Ngugi believes that one of the damaging results of colonialism is that it bequeathed to African society leaders who have no sense of identity or direction. These are elites who have uncritically accepted the Western worldview and are already enjoying the greatest social status, wealth and power in society. As such they are too complacent to pursue any fundamental structural changes that might reintegrate the masses. Instead, state officials use the powerful instruments of economic control inherited from colonial regimes to serve the interest of their fellow elites and themselves. Rather than pursuing policies that will ensure good governance, the ruling class ends up as part of the problem hindering Africa's political development. The situation is exacerbated by continuous absorption of more elites in bureaucratic employment. It is only the oppressed who have not been corrupted by power and its many privileges who can bring about responsible and accountable government. The solution lies in the oppressed coming together to dismantle state power and replacing it with a central authority. There is need for collective action and central monitoring to engender a strong communal consciousness and promote universal participation. Moreover, this will help restore, so Ngugi believes, a vital advantage of African traditional societies, whereby there is communal sharing and the haves take care of the have-nots through defined, accepted and acceptable institutional frameworks.

For Achebe, the issue of finding the right calibre of people to manage state affairs is all-important in resolving Africa's problems. To institute accountable government, leaders need to abdicate their sense of superiority over the people they govern. Rulers need to 're-establish vital inner links with the poor and dispossessed' in society. This does not, however, mean handing over complete authority to the state to moderate all the affairs of the individual. What is needed are elites who can act as role models.

There is an air of suffocation associated with the notion of the state taking over the control of all aspects of life in society. The likelihood of people's consent being trampled upon under a communist regime is high. By entrusting to the state the responsibility of knowing what is right for the individual, the individual is denied a fundamental right to map out his or her own way of life, trust his or her own judgement and act on the basis of conviction and practical knowledge. Besides, progress in many fields depends on holding our ideals and views open to public criticism.

Far from acting in the public interest, authoritarian regimes end up separating leaders from the led and invariably inflict pain on people. Even ending class exploitation has some crucial demerits. To eliminate class will amount to eradicating an important legitimate ground for conflict. The point is that conflict is important in evaluating the merits of opposing positions, proffering counter-opinions on the best course of action to take, and in promoting tolerance.

Nevertheless, Achebe's position fails in some important respects. He appears to take it for granted that the elites, due to their expert knowledge, must be best qualified to rule. The point, however, is that 'to govern a state well takes more than knowledge' (Dahl 1998: 73). It calls for more steely qualities, such as 'incorruptibility, a firm resistance to all the enormous temptations of power, a continuing and inflexible dedication to the public good rather than benefits for oneself or one's groups' (ibid.). Given that the elite are from the privileged class who are part of the institutional problem, the feasibility of their embarking on real transformation that will render them accountable to the people is in serious doubt.

Besides, Achebe underrates the role of civil society in the maintenance of democratic order. For democratic regulation of life to take root it requires a strong civil society, an organized citizenry aware of their rights and able and willing to defend and protect them. In a situation such as obtains in most African countries, where the people allow the leaders to use them as political thugs, and even religious thugs, to fight their opponents and consolidate their positions and privileges, it will be difficult for people not to be exploited. In Nigeria, for instance, the violence that occurs almost daily between militant groups, youth organizations and religious fanatics is in most cases designed to safeguard the interests of the leaders.

Irrespective of the huge discrepancies in power, wealth, material possessions, opportunities and privileges, some people are happy to be associated with a leader who once in a while makes it possible for them to obtain government contracts and other material help. This makes it difficult for them to work towards fostering the strong civic consciousness necessary for building a united political community. The point is that civil society in most African countries is still very weak. People are exploited because they are exploitable. The problem goes beyond Achebe's view that 'Nigerians [Africans] are what they are only because their leaders are *not* what *they* should be' (Achebe 1983: 10).

The issue, actually, is that the attitudes of the leaders are determined by what the people are willing to take and what they are not ready to take. It is the people's conduct and actions that determine the kinds of social structure and societal values that are predominant in society. Once the people realize that *ultimately* they are the protectors of their own rights, the leaders are bound to sit up and take notice. It took the French Revolution to overthrow the French monarchy and abolish or radically alter many of the laws, institutions and ideas associated with it.

Moreover, even if leaders are able to act as role models, creating a better society will still depend on the receptivity of the people to the positive attributes of their leaders. Without the people's willingness to imbibe and practise the exemplary conduct of their leaders, it will be almost impossible to transform society. From whatever angle the issue is approached, the role of civil society in achieving an enduring social transformation is fundamental.

All in all, to ensure political accountability requires tolerance, an independent judiciary that has the power to subject public officers to the law, a free press willing and able to expose official misdeeds, and an organized citizenry aware of their rights and willing to claim them whenever necessary, even by petitioning the government. This will also help in checking the trend towards political fanaticism that is becoming a common feature in many African societies. This is not to say that liberal freedom cannot be excessive. There is a need for the state to exert sufficient authority to ensure that people do not abuse their liberty, and that people's actions conform to, and are responsive to other community interests.

Conclusion

In the final analysis, it is necessary to be mindful of the fluid nature of politics and the need to be guided in decisions by changing circumstances and their long-term implications. Transformation of African societies will depend largely on the adoption of ideologies that are balanced enough to remain stable in the face of unforeseen events, and on the ability of leaders to approach power and authority from a service-oriented perspective and a committed willingness to work within the political currents and conditions unique to the circumstances of particular African states.

Lastly, what is important in studying Achebe's and Ngugi's proposals is to show the significant contributions they have added – indeed, literature as a whole makes – to the promotion of African self-understanding by providing an intellectual and analytical framework within which the African political experience can be conceptualized, interpreted and reorganized.

Notes

2 Literature as philosophy: a theoretical framework

1 Karl Marx, 'Theses on Feuerbach' (Marx and Engels 1968: 30).

2 Chinua Achebe, 'The African Writer and the Biafran Cause' (Achebe 1975: 78).

3 T. S. Eliot, 'Burnt Norton' (Eliot 1974: 193).

4 This book endorses the arguments put forward in defence of a philosophically oriented political theory. See L. S. Rathore (1975, 1976) and his 'Political Theory: A Quest for Reconciliation', *Indian Journal of Political Science*, XXXVIII(1), January–March 1977.

5 Sabine used political theory to mean political philosophy.

6 This issue has divided political philosophers into camps. The two most opposed are the communitarians and the universalists. It is the position of this book that while political philosophers may reflect values and assumptions of a given community, their philosophies still have value for the entire human race. Plato's political philosophy, shaped largely by the social disintegration in his beloved Athens and the manner of Socrates' death, still has value for us if we reflect on some of the questions he raised: about the true aims of the society, the nature of justice, the best way individuals can develop both for themselves and society.

7 See Simon Gikandi, 'The Political Novel' (Gikandi 1987) and Jude Aighe Agho, 'Anger and Beyond: Three Novels of Sembene Ousmane' (Agho 1995).

8 See Green (1986); Gikandi (1987); Sole (1988).

9 See Albert Olu Ashaolu (1986) and Jude Aighe Agho, 'Revolutionary Imperatives in the Novels of Ayi Kwei Armah' (Agho 1995).

3 Chinua Achebe and Ngugi wa Thiong'o as political thinkers

1 Aristotle, 'The Natural Basis of Society', from *Politics*, in Ayer (1946: 158).

2 Niccolo Machiavelli, 'Rulers Must Calculate', from *The Prince*, in Ayer (1946: 170).

3 Thomas Hobbes, 'The Basis of Sovereign Authority', from *De Cive*, in Ayer (1946: 175).

4 John Locke, 'Natural Rights and Civil Society', from *Treatise of Civil Government*, in Ayer (1946: 195).

5 Chinua Achebe, 'The Novelist as Teacher', in Achebe (1988: 30).

6 Chinua Achebe, 'Colonialist Criticism', in Achebe (1988: 57).

7 Chinua Achebe, 'The African Writer and the Biafran Cause', in Achebe (1975: 78–84).

4 Achebe's reformist agenda in *Anthills of the Savannah*

1 See Immanuel Wallerstein, 'Dependence in an Interdependent World: The Limited Possibilities of Transformation within the Capitalist World-Economy', in Wallerstein (1979).

5 Ngugi's Marxist aesthetics

1 Frederick Engels, 'Speech at the Graveside of Karl Marx', in Marx and Engels (1968: 429).

2 Karl Marx, 'Theses on Feuerbach' (ibid.: 30).

3 Frederick Engels, 'Engels to W. Borgius in Breslau' (ibid.: 694).

4 Jean-Paul Sartre, 'Introduction', in Fanon (1967: 19).

5 Ime Ikiddeh, 'Foreword', in Ngugi (1972: xiv).

6 Achebe and Ngugi on the African condition

1 Marx and Engels, 'Manifesto of the Communist Party', in Marx and Engels (1968: 35).

2 Frederick Engels, 'The Origin of the Family, Private Property and the State', in Marx and Engels (ibid.: 528).

3 Frederick Engels, 'Letter to A. Bebel', in Marx and Engels (ibid.: 335).

4 Karl Marx, 'Critique of the Gotha Programme', in Marx and Engels (ibid.: 327).

7 Which way for Africa?

1 See Dahl (1998). For Dahl effective participation refers to the equal and effective opportunities of all members to make their views known regarding any policy before it can be adopted. Voting equality has to do with the right of all members to an equal and effective opportunity to vote and for all votes to be counted as equal. Enlightened understanding points to the right of each member to be properly educated on the policy under consideration, alternatives to the policy and their likely consequences. Control of the agenda refers to the right to have the opportunity to decide how and what matters are to be placed on the agenda. Inclusion of adults means that with the exception of transients and persons proved incapable of caring for themselves, all adults subject to the laws of the state should have the full rights of citizens implied by the first four criteria.

2 Marx and Engels, 'Manifesto of the Communist Party', in Marx and Engels (1968: 53).

Bibliography

Abraham, Peter (1955), 'The Conflict of Culture in Africa', *Phyllon*, XVI(4).

Achebe, Chinua (1958), *Things Fall Apart*, London: Heinemann.

— (1960), *No Longer at Ease*, London: Heinemann.

— (1964), *Arrow of God*, Ibadan: Heinemann.

— (1966), *A Man of the People*, London: Heinemann.

— (1975), *Morning Yet on Creation Day*, London: Heinemann.

— (1983), *The Trouble with Nigeria*, Enugu, Nigeria: Fourth Dimension Publishers.

— (1987), *Anthills of the Savannah*, London: Heinemann.

— (1988), *Hopes and Impediments: Selected Essays 1965–1987*, London, Heinemann International.

Acton, H. B. (1972), *The Illusion of the Epoch: Marxism–Leninism as a Philosophical Creed*, London and Boston, MA: Routledge and Kegan Paul.

Adeniran, Tunde (1994), *The Politics of Soyinka*, Ibadan: Fountain Publications.

Agho, Jude Aigbe (1995), *Standpoints on the African Novel*, Ibadan: Sam Bookman.

Aina, Tade Akin (1997), *Globalization and Social Policy in Africa: Issues and Research Directions*, Dakar, Senegal: Codesria.

Ake, Claude (1979), *Social Science as Imperialism: A Theory of Political Development*, Ibadan: Ibadan University Press.

— (1981), *A Political Economy of Africa*, London: Longman.

— (1992), 'Devaluing Democracy', *Journal of Democracy*, 3(3), July.

— (1994), *Democratization of Disempowerment in Africa*, Lagos: Malthouse Press.

— (1996), *Is Africa Democratizing?*, Lagos: Malthouse Press.

— (2001), *Democracy and Development in Africa*, Ibadan: Spectrum Books.

Akiwowo, A. A. and Richard Olaniyan (1985), 'Social Change and Stability in Contemporary Nigeria', in Richard Olaniyan (ed.), *Nigerian History and Culture*, Nigeria: Longman.

Allen, V. L. (1972), 'The Meaning of the Working Class in Africa', *Journal of Modern African Studies*, 10(2), July.

Amuta, Chidi (1989), *The Theory of African Literature: Implications for Practical Criticism*, London and New Jersey: Institute for African Alternatives and Zed Books.

— (1995), 'Fanon, Cabral and Ngugi on National Liberation', in Bill Ashcroft et al. (eds), *The Post Colonial Studies Reader*, London and New York: Routledge.

Aristotle (1965a), *Politics*, trans. Benjamin Jowett, ed. H. W. C. Davis, Oxford: Clarendon Press.

— (1965b), 'On the Art of Poetry', in T. S. Dorsch (trans.),

Classical Literary Criticism, Harmondsworth: Penguin Books.

Armah, Ayi Kwei (1969), *The Beautyful Ones are Not Yet Born*, London: Heinemann.

Arrighi, Giovanni (2002), ' The African Crisis', *New Left Review*, 15, May–June.

Asante, S. K. B. (1991), *African Development: Adebayo Adedeji's Alternative Strategies*, Ibadan: Spectrum Books.

Ashaolu, Olu (1986), 'A Vision of Society: The Novels of Ayi Kwei Armah', in S. O. Asein and A. O. Ashaolu (eds), *Studies in the African Novel*, Vol. I, Ibadan: Ibadan University Press.

Ayer, A. J. (1946), *Language, Truth and Logic*, New York: Dover Publications.

— (1956), *The Problem of Knowledge*, Harmondsworth: Penguin Books.

— (1976), *The Central Questions of Philosophy*, Harmondsworth: Pelican Books.

Bakhurst, David (1998), 'Marxist Philosophy, Russian and Soviet', in Edward Craig (ed.), *Routledge Encyclopedia of Philosophy*, Vol. 6, London and New York: Routledge.

Balibar, Etienne and Pierre Macherey (1992), 'On Literature as an Ideological Form', in Francis Mulhern (ed.), *Contemporary Marxist Literary Criticism*, London and New York: Longman.

Barker, Francis et al. (eds) (1986), *Literature, Politics and Theory: Papers from the Essex Conference 1976–84*, London and New York: Methuen.

Baxter, Joan (2002), 'Burying Capitalism', *BBC Focus on Africa*, April–June.

Beiner, Ronald (1992), *What's the Matter with Liberalism*, Berkeley: University of California Press.

Bell, Richard H. (1989), 'Narratives in African Philosophy', *Philosophy*, 64(249), July.

Bellamy, Richard (1999), *Liberalism and Pluralism: Towards a Politics of Compromise*, London and New York: Routledge.

Berger, Peter L. (1992), 'The Uncertain Triumph of Democratic Capitalism', *Journal of Democracy*, 3(3), July.

Bhagwati, Jagdish (1992), 'Democracy and Development', *Journal of Democracy*, 3(3), July.

Bodunrin, P. O. (1981a), 'The Question of African Philosophy', *Philosophy*, 56.

— (1981b), 'Philosophy: Meaning and Method', *Ibadan Journal of Humanistic Studies*, 1, April.

Botchwey, Kwesi (1977), 'Marxism and the Analysis of the African Reality', *Africa Development*, II(1).

Boulton, Marjorie (1960), *The Anatomy of Drama*, London: Routledge and Kegan Paul.

Brett, E. A. (1973), *Colonialism and Underdevelopment in East Africa*, New York: Nok Publishers.

Brown, Nicholas (1999), 'Revolution and Recidivism: The Problem of Kenya History in the Plays of Ngugi wa Thiong'o', *Research in African Literatures: Drama and Performance*, 30(4), Winter.

Bunce, Valerie (2001), 'The Postsocialist Experience and Comparative Politics', *Political Science and Politics*, XXXIV(4), December.

Caron, B., A. Gboyega and E. Osaghae (eds) (1992),

Democratic Transition in Africa, Ibadan: CREDU, June.

Carrol, David (1990), *Chinua Achebe: Novelist, Poet, Critic* (2nd edn), Houndmills: Macmillan Press.

Carroll, Andrew et al. (eds) (1998), *101 Great American Poems*, Mineola, New York: Dover Publications.

Caute, David (1978), 'Introduction', in Jean-Paul Sartre, *What is Literature?* (trans. Bernard Frechtman), Guildford: Methuen & Co.

Chabal, Patrick and Jean-Pascal Daloz (1999), *Africa Works: Disorder as Political Instrument*, Oxford: James Currey; Bloomington and Indianapolis: Indiana University Press.

Chapman, Michael (2003), *Southern African Literatures*, Pietermaritzburg: University of Natal Press.

Charney, Evan (1998), 'Political Liberalism, Deliberative Democracy, and the Public Sphere', *American Political Science Review*, 92(1), March.

Chazan, Naomi, P. Lewis, R. Mortimer, D. Rothchild and S. John Stedman (1999), *Politics and Society in Contemporary Africa* (3rd edn), Boulder, CO: Lynne Rienner.

Clapham, Christopher (1970), 'The Context of African Political Thought', *Journal of Modern African Studies*, 8(1).

— (1985), *Third World Politics: An Introduction*, USA and Canada: University of Wisconsin Press.

Clarke, J. J. (1971), '"The End of History": A Reappraisal of Marx's Views on Alienation and Human Emancipation', *Canadian Journal of Political Science*, IV (3), September.

Costello, Edward B. (1963), 'Marx, Karl', *The American People's Encyclopedia*, Vol. 13, New York: Grolier Incorporated.

Costello, Jacqueline and Amy Tucker (1989), *Forms of Literature: A Writer's Collection*, New York: Random House.

Cruickshank, John (1962), 'Some Aspects of French Fiction 1935–1960', in John Cruickshank (ed.), *The Novelist as Philosopher*, London: Oxford University Press.

Curtis, Ernst Robert (1953), *European Literature and the Latin Middle Ages* (trans. Willard R. Trask), New York and Evanston, IL: Harper and Row.

Dada, Pius Olusegun (1986), 'The Tradition of the African Novel', in S. O. Asein and A. O. Ashaolu (eds), *Studies in the African Novel*, Vol. I, Ibadan: Ibadan University Press.

Dahl, Robert A. (1998), *On Democracy*, New Haven, CT and London: Yale University Press.

Daniels, Robert V. (1997), 'Marxism', *The Encyclopedia Americana* (international edn), Vol. 18, Danbury, CT: Grolier Incorporated.

Danto, Arthur C. (1985), 'Philosophy as/and/of Literature', in J. Rajchman and C. West (eds), *Post Analytic Philosophy*, New York: Columbia University Press.

De Sauvigny, De Bertier G. (1970), 'Liberalism, Nationalism and Socialism: The Birth of Three Words', *Review of Politics*, 32(2), April.

Descartes, René (1997), 'First Meditation' (trans. Elizabeth S.

Haldene and G. R. T. Ross), in Enrique Chavez–Arvizo (ed.), *Descartes' Key Philosophical Writings*, Hertfordshire: Wordsworth Classics of World Literature.

Diamond, Larry (1989), 'Fiction as Political Thought', *African Affairs: The Journal of the Royal African Society*, 88(352), July.

— (1993), 'Three Paradoxes of Democracy', in Larry Diamond and Marc F. Plattner (eds), *The Global Resurgence of Democracy*, Baltimore, PA and London: Johns Hopkins University Press.

Diop, David (1976), 'The Vultures', in K. E. Senanu and T. Vincent (eds), *A Selection of African Poetry*, London: Longman.

Diquattro, Arthur (1998), 'Liberal Theory and the Idea of Communist Justice', *American Political Science Review*, 92(1), March.

Dobb, Maurice (1952), 'The Accumulation of Capital', *Modern Quarterly*, 7(2), Spring.

Dryzek, John S. and Jeffrey Berejikian (1993), 'Reconstructive Democratic Theory', *American Political Science Review*, 87(1), March.

Duncan, Graeme (1988), 'Political Obligation: Some Sceptical Views', in G. H. R. Parkinson (ed.), *An Encyclopaedia of Philosophy*, London: Routledge.

Dunton, Chris (1992), *Make Man Talk True: Nigerian Drama in English Since 1970*, London: Hans Zell Publishers.

Eagleton, Terry (1991), *Ideology: An Introduction*, London and New York: Verso.

Echeruo, M. J. C. (1975), 'Chinua Achebe', in Bruce King and Kolawole Ogungbesan (eds), *A Celebration of Black and African Writing*, Zaria: Ahmadu Bello University Press; Oxford, London: Oxford University Press.

Edman, Irwin (1957), 'Philosophy and the Literary Artist', in Stanley Romaine Hopper (ed.), *Spiritual Problems in Contemporary Literature*, New York: Harper and Brothers.

Ehling, Holger G. (ed.) (1991), 'Critical Approaches to *Anthills of the Savannah*', *Matatu*, 8.

Ekaney, Nkwelle (1980), 'Corruption and Politics in Chinua Achebe's *A Man of the People*: An Assessment', *Présence Africaine*, 115, 3rd Quarterly.

Ekeh, Peter P. (1983), *Colonialism and Social Structure*, Ibadan: Ibadan University Press.

Eliot, T. S. (1974), *Collected Poems: 1902–1962*, London: Faber and Faber.

Enekwe, Onuora Ossie (1996), 'We are All Learning from History: Interview with Ngugi wa Thiong'o', *Glendora Review*, 1(3).

Eyol, Hansel Ndumbe (1986), 'Theatre of Relevance: An Interview with Ngugi wa Thiong'o', *African Theatre Review*, 1(2), April.

Ezenwa-Ohaeto (1997), *Chinua Achebe: A Biography*, Oxford: James Currey; Bloomington and Indianapolis: Indiana University Press.

Falck, Colin (1988), 'Fictions and Reality', *Philosophy: The Journal of the Royal Institute of Philosophy*, 63(245), July.

Fanon, F. (1967), *The Wretched of the Earth*, Harmondsworth: Penguin Books.

Farrington, Benjamin (1952), 'Karl Marx – Scholar and Revolutionary', *Modern Quarterly*, 7(2), Spring.

Flower, Roger (1991), 'Literature', in Martin Coyle et al. (eds), *Encyclopedia of Literature and Criticism*, London: Routledge.

Flynn, Thomas R. (1994), 'Philosophy of Existence 2: Sartre', in Richard Kearney (ed.), *Routledge History of Philosophy Vol. VIII: Twentieth-century Continental Philosophy*, London and New York: Routledge.

Frow, John (1991), 'Marxist Criticism', in Martin Coyle et al. (eds), *Encyclopedia of Literature and Criticism*, London: Routledge.

Fukuyama, Francis (1992a), *The End of History and the Last Man*, New York: Avon Books.

— (1992b), 'Capitalism and Democracy: The Missing Link', *Journal of Democracy*, 3(3), July.

Gakwandi, Shatto Arthur (1977), *The Novel and Contemporary Experience in Africa*, London: Heinemann; New York: Africana Publishing Company.

Galtung, Johan (2000), 'Leaving Behind a Century of Violence', *Journal of Future Studies*, 4(2), May.

Gamble, Andrew (1981), *An Introduction to Modern Social and Political Thought*, Houndsmills: Macmillan Education.

Gandhi, Mohandas K. (2000), 'Means and Ends', in Gail M. Presbey et al. (eds), *The Philosophical Quest: A Cross-cultural Reader*, Boston, MA: McGraw Hill.

Gbadegesin, Segun (1997), 'Current Trends and Perspectives in African Philosophy', in Eliot Deutsch and Ron Bontekoe (eds), *A Companion to World Philosophies*, Malden: Blackwell Publishers.

Giddens, Anthony (1971), *Capitalism and Modern Social Theory: An Analysis of the Writings of Marx, Durkheim and Max Weber*, Cambridge: Cambridge University Press.

Gikandi, Simon (1987), *Reading the African Novel*, Oxford: James Currey; Nairobi: Heinemann Kenya; Portsmouth, NH: Heinemann.

— (1991), 'Literature in Africa (1960–90)', *Africa Today* (2nd edn), London: Africa Books.

Goldie, Terry (1981), 'African Literature Today', *Canadian Journal of African Studies*, 15(3).

Gooding-Williams, Robert (1986), 'Literary Fiction as Philosophy: The Case of Nietzsche's Zarathustra', *Journal of Philosophy*, LXXXIII(11), November.

Grant, R. A. D. (1988), 'Defenders of the State', in G. H. R. Parkinson (ed.), *An Encyclopaedia of Philosophy*, London: Routledge.

Green, Reginald H. (1965), 'Four African Development Plans: Ghana, Kenya, Nigeria, and Tanzania', *Journal of Modern African Studies*, 3(2), August.

Green, Robert (1986), 'The Politics of Subversion: Alex La Guma's *In the Fog of the Season's End*', in S. O. Asein and A. O. Ashaolu (eds), *Studies in the African Novel*, Vol. 1, Ibadan: Ibadan University Press.

Gugelberger, Georg M. (1985), 'Marxist Literary Debates and

Their Continuity in African Literary Criticism', in Georg M. Gugelberger (ed.), *Marxism and African Literature*, Oxford: James Currey.

Gunnell, John G. (1979), 'Philosophy and Political Theory', *Government and Opposition: A Journal of Comparative Politics*, 14(2), Spring.

Hanson, David W. (1979), 'What is Living and What is Dead in Liberalism?', *American Politics Quarterly*, 2(1), January.

Harries, Karsten (1986), 'Boundary Disputes', *Journal of Philosophy*, LXXXIII(11), November.

Harris, Ian (1996), 'Locke's Political Theory', in Stuart Brown (ed.), *Routledge History of Philosophy: British Philosophy and the Age of Enlightenment*, Vol. V, London and New York: Routledge.

Hart, W. A. (1972), 'The Philosopher's Interest in African Thought: A Synopsis', *Second Order: An African Journal of Philosophy*, 1(1), January.

Held, David (1987), *Models of Democracy*, Stanford, CA: Stanford University Press.

Henshaw, Ene James (1956), *This is Our Chance*, London: Hodder and Stoughton.

Hetherington, Marc J. (1998), 'The Political Relevance of Political Trust', *American Political Science Review*, 92(4), December.

Hobbes, Thomas (1946), 'The Basis of Sovereign Authority', from *De cive*, in A. J. Ayer (ed.), *Language, Truth and Logic*, New York: Dover Publications.

Holmquist, Frank and Ayuka Oendo (2001), 'Kenya: Democracy, Decline, and Despair', *Current History: A Journal of Contemporary World Affairs*, 100(646), May.

Hountondji, Paulin J. (1983), *African Philosophy: Myth and Reality*, London: Hutchinson University Library for Africa.

Huntington, Samuel P. (1991), *The Third Wave: Democratization in the Late Twentieth Century*, Norman: University of Oklahoma Press.

Hyden, Goran (2001), 'Africanists' Contributions to Political Science', *Political Science and Politics*, XXXIV(4), December.

Ihonvbere, Julius (ed.) (1989), *The Political Economy of Crisis and Under-development in Africa: Selected Works of Claude Ake*, Lagos, Nigeria: Jad Publishers.

Ikiddeh, Ime (1975), 'Ngugi wa Thiong'o: The Novelist as Historian', in Bruce King and Kolawole Ogungbesan (eds), *A Celebration of Black and African Writing*, Zaria: Ahmadu Bello University Press; London: Oxford University Press

— (1986), 'Ideology and Revolutionary Action in the Contemporary African Novel', in S. O. Asein and A. O. Ashaolu (eds), *Studies in the African Novel*, Vol. 1, Ibadan: Ibadan University Press.

Innes, C. L. (1990), *Chinua Achebe*, Cambridge: Cambridge University Press.

Irele, Abiola (1981), *The African Experience in Literature and Ideology*, London: Heinemann.

Jameson, Fredric (1981), *The Political Unconscious: Narrative as a Socially Symbolic Act*, Ithaca, NY: Cornell University Press.

Jefferson, Thomas (1963), 'The Declaration of Independence',

The United States in Literature,
Chicago, IL: Scott, Foresman and
Company.

Jinadu, Adele L. (1980), *Fanon: In
Search of the African Revolution*,
Enugu, Nigeria: Fourth
Dimension Publishers.

Joseph, Richard (1991), 'Africa: The
Rebirth of Political Freedom',
Journal of Democracy, 2(4), Fall.

— (1998), 'Africa, 1990–1997: From
Abertura to Closure', *Journal of
Democracy*, 9(2), April.

Kamenju, Grant (1985), '"Petals
of Blood" as a Mirror of the
African Revolution', in Georg
M. Gugelberger (ed.), *Marxism
and African Literature*, Oxford:
James Currey.

Keat, Russell and John O'Neill
(1998), 'Socialism', in Edward
Craig (ed.), *Routledge
Encyclopedia of Philosophy*,
Vol. 8, London and New York:
Routledge.

Kim, Kyung-won (1992), 'Marx,
Schumpeter, and the East
Asian Experience', *Journal of
Democracy*, 3(3), July.

Klugmann, James (1952), 'The
Peaceful Co-existence of
Capitalism and Socialism',
Modern Quarterly, 7(2), Spring.

Knight, Everett W. (1962), *Literature
Considered as Philosophy*, New
York: Collier Books.

Konstantinov, F. V. et al. (1982),
*The Fundamentals of Marxist-
Leninist Philosophy*, Moscow:
Progress Publishers.

Kopoka, Peter Anthony (2001),
'Poverty and Unemployement in
Tanzania', *International Journal
of African Studies*, 3(1), Fall.

Kortenaar, Neil Ten (1993), '"Only
Connect": *Anthills of the
Savannah* and Achebe's *Trouble*

with Nigeria', *Research in
African Literatures*, 24(3), Fall.

Kullberg, Judith S. and William
Zimmermann (1999), 'Liberal
Elites, Socialist Masses, and
Problems of Russian Democracy',
World Politics, 51(3), Autumn.

La Guma, Alex (1972), *In the Fog
of the Season's End*, London:
Heinemann.

Laing, Dave (1978), *The Marxist
Theory of Art: An Introductory
Survey*, Sussex, England:
Harvester Press; Boulder, CO:
Westview Press.

Langdon, Steve (1975),
'Multinational Corporations,
Taste Transfer and Under-
development: A Case Study from
Kenya', *RAPE*, 2.

Lefever, Ernest W. (1970), *Spear
and Sceptre: Army, Police and
Parliament in Tropical Africa*,
Washington, DC: Brookings
Institution.

Lenin, V. I. (1965), *The State and
Revolution* (rev. edn), Moscow:
Progress Publishers.

— (1993), 'Imperialism, the Highest
Form of Capitalism', in Howard
Williams et al. (eds), *A Reader
in International Relations and
Political Theory*, Buckingham:
Open University Press.

Leys, Colin (1965), 'What is the
Problem About Corruption?',
*Journal of Modern African
Studies*, 3(2), August.

Lindfors, Bernth (ed.) (1985),
'Special Issue on Ngugi wa
Thiong'o', *Research in African
Literatures*, 16(2), Summer.

Lloyd, Robert B. (2002), 'Zimbabwe:
The Making of an Autocratic
"Democracy"', *Current History:
A Journal of Contemporary
World Affairs*, 101(655), May.

Locke, John (1946), 'Natural Rights and Civil Society', from *Treatise of Civil Government*, in A. J. Ayer (ed.), *Language, Truth and Logic*, New York: Dover Publications.

— (1947), *An Essay Concerning Human Understanding*, London: J. M. Dent and Sons.

Lowenthal, Leo (1961), *Literature, Popular Culture and Society*, Englewood Cliffs, NJ: Prentice-Hall.

Lugard, Frederick D. (1968), *The Rise of Our East African Empire*, Vol. 1, London: Frank Cass.

McGeary, Johanna (1999), 'Mohandas Gandhi', *Time*, 31 December.

Mclellan, David (1980), *The Thought of Karl Marx* (2nd edn), London and Basingstoke: Macmillan.

Machiavelli, Niccolo (1946), 'Rulers Must Calculate', from *The Prince*, in A. J. Ayer, *Language Truth and Logic*, New York: Dover Publications.

Maja-Pearce, Adewale (1992), *A Mask Dancing: Nigerian Novelists in the Eighties*, London: Hans Zell Publishers.

Mamdani, Mahmood (2002), *Citizen and Subject: Contemporary Africa and the Legacy of Late Colonialism*, Ibadan: John Archers; Kampala: Fountain Publishers; Cape Town: David Philip; Oxford: James Currey.

Mandela, Nelson (1999), 'Gandhi: Warrior', *Time*, 31 December.

Marx, Karl (1956), *Selected Writings in Sociology and Social Philosophy*, T. B. Bottomore and Maximilien Rubel (eds), Harmondsworth: Penguin Books.

Marx, Karl and Frederick Engels (1968), *Selected Works*, Moscow: Progress Publishers.

Mason, F. T. (1982), 'Towards an Agenda for Philosophers in Africa Today', *Uche*, 6.

Mayhead, Robin (1965), *Understanding Literature*, Cambridge: Cambridge University Press.

Mbembe, Achille (1992), 'The Banality of Power and the Aesthetics of Vulgarity in the Postcolony', *Public Culture*, 4(2), Spring.

Memmi, Albert (1981), 'The Coloniser and the Colonised', in Dennis L. Cohen and John Daniel (eds), *Political Economy of Africa*, Harlow: Longman.

Miliband, Ralph (1992), 'The Socialist Alternative', *Journal of Democracy*, 3(3), July.

Miller, David (1998), 'Political Philosophy', in Edward Craig (ed.), *Routledge Encyclopedia of Philosophy*, Vol. 7, London and New York: Routledge.

Mitchell, Julian (1973), 'Truth and Fiction', *Philosophy and the Arts: Royal Institute of Philosophy Lectures 1971–1972*, Vol. 6, London: Macmillan.

Mouralis, Bernard (1995), 'Literature and Philosophy in French-speaking Africa', in Anthony Kirk Greene and Daniel Bach (eds), *State and Society in Francophone Africa Since Independence*, New York: St Martin's Press.

Muller, Edward N. and Mitchell A. Seligson (1994), 'Civic Culture and Democracy: The Question of Causal Relationships', *American Political Science Review*, 88(3), September.

Mutiso, G.-C.M. (1974), *Socio-political Thought in African Literature: Weusi?*, London: Macmillan.

Nazareth, Peter (1985), 'The Second Homecoming: Multiple Ngugis in "Petals of Blood"', in Georg M. Gugelberger (ed.), *Marxism and African Literature*, Oxford: James Currey.

Ngugi wa Thiong'o (1964), *Weep Not, Child*, Ibadan: Heinemann.

— (1965), *The River Between*, London: Heinemann.

— (1967), *A Grain of Wheat*, London: Heinemann.

— (1972), *Homecoming: Essays on Africa and Caribbean Literature, Culture and Politics*, London: Heinemann.

— (1977), *Petals of Blood*, Nigeria: Heinemann Educational Books.

— (1981), *Writers in Politics*, London: Heinemann.

— (1982), *Devil on the Cross*, London: Heinemann.

— (1986), *Decolonising the Mind: The Politics of Language in African Literature*, Oxford: James Currey; Nairobi: Heinemann Kenya; Portsmouth NH: Heinemann.

— (1993), *Moving the Centre: The Struggle for Cultural Freedoms*, Oxford: James Currey; Nairobi: EAEP; Portsmouth, NH: Heinemann.

Nisbet, Robert (1982), *The Social Philosophers: Community and Conflict in Western Thought*, New York: Washington Square Press.

Njoku, David (2000), 'Running', *Little Drops 2: An Anthology of Contemporary Nigerian Short Stories*, Ibadan: Spectrum Books.

Nkosi, Lewis (1981), *Tasks and Masks*, Harlow: Longman.

Nkrumah, Kwame (1965), *Neo-Colonialism: The Last Stage of Imperialism*, London: Panaf.

Nnolim, Charles E. (1992), *Approaches to the African Novel: Essays in Analysis*, London: Saros International Publishers.

Nobilo, Mario (1992), 'Problems of Political Stability and Internal Unity of African Countries', in Abiola Irele (ed.), *African Education and Identity: Proceedings of the 5th Session of the International Congress of African Studies Held at Ibadan, December, 1985*, London: Hans Zell Publishers; Ibadan: Spectrum Books.

Norris, Christopher (1991), 'Criticism', in Martin Coyle et al. (eds), *Encyclopedia of Literature and Criticism*, London: Routledge.

Novak, Michael (1969), 'Philosophy and Fiction', in Jerry H. Gill (ed.), *Philosophy Today*, No. 2, London: Collier-Macmillan.

Nwoga, Ibe D. (1981), 'The Igbo World of Achebe's *Arrow of God*', *Research in African Literatures*, 12(1), Spring.

Nwosu, Maik (1997), 'The Honourable Fartheads', in Maik Nwosu, *Return to Algadez*, Lagos: Malthouse Press.

— (1998), *Suns of Kush*, Lagos: Malthouse Press.

Nyerere, Julius (1998), 'Leaders Must Not be Masters', in Emmanual Chukwudi Eze (ed.), *African Philosophy: An Anthology*, Malden, MA: Blackwell Publishers.

Nzongola-Ntalaja (1987), *Revolution and Counter-revolution in Africa: Essays in Contemporary Politics*, London and New Jersey: Institute for African Alternatives and Zed Books.

Ogbaa, Kalu (1981), 'An Interview

with Chinua Achebe', *Research in African Literatures*, 12(1), Spring.

Oguejiofor, Obi J. (2000), 'In Search of the Democratic Ideal', *Current Viewpoint: A Review of Culture and Society*, 2(1, 2).

Ogunjimi, Bayo (1994), 'What is Literature?', in Olu Obafemi (ed.), *New Introduction to Literature*, Ibadan: Y Books.

Ojinmah Umelo (1991), *Chinua Achebe: New Perspectives*, Ibadan: Spectrum Books.

Ojukwu, Emeka (1969), *The Ahiara Declaration: The Principles of the Biafran Revolution*, Geneva, Switzerland: Markpress.

Okigbo, Christopher (1971), *Labyrinths: with Path of Thunder*, London: Heinemann.

Oladipo, Olusegun (1993), *Philosophy, Literature and the African Novel*, Ibadan: Options Book and Information Services.

— (2001), *Political Concepts and Ideologies*, Vol. 2, Ibadan, Nigeria: Hope Publications.

Olafson, Frederick A. (1967), 'Santayana, George', in Paul Edwards (ed.), *The Encyclopedia of Philosophy*, Vol. 7, New York: Macmillan.

Omoregbe, Joseph I. (1985), 'African Philosophy: Yesterday and Today', in P. O. Bodunrin (ed.), *Philosophy in Africa: Trends and Perspectives*, Ile-Ife, Nigeria: University of Ife Press.

Omoruyi, Omo, D. Schlosser, A. Sambo and A. Okwuosa (eds) (1994), *Democratisation in Africa: African Perspectives*, Vol. 1, Benin City, Nigeria: Hima and Hima.

Omotoso, Kole (1996), *Achebe or Soyinka?: A Study in Contrasts*, London: Hans Zell Publishers.

Onoge, Omafume F. (1985a), 'The Crisis of Consciousness in Modern African Literature', in Georg M. Gugelberger (ed.), *Marxism and African Literature*, Oxford: James Currey.

— (1985b), 'Towards a Marxist Sociology of African Literature', in Georg M. Gugelberger (ed.), *Marxism and African Literature*, Oxford: James Currey.

Onwudiwe, Ebere (2002), 'Africa's Other Story', *Current History: A Journal of Contemporary World Affairs*, 101(655), May.

Opata, Damian U. and Aloysius U. Ohaegbu (eds) (2002), *Major Themes in African Literature*, Nsukka: AP Express.

Oruka, Odera H. (1975), 'The Fundamental Principles in the Question of "African Philosophy": Part 1: The Meaning of African Philosophy', *Second Order: An African Journal of Philosophy*, IV(1), January.

— (1978), 'African Philosophy: An Introduction', *Second Order: An African Journal of Philosophy*, VII(1, 2), January–July.

Orwell, George (1949), *Nineteen Eighty-Four*, New York: Harcourt, Brace and Company.

Osaghae, E. (1993), 'Colonialism and African Political Thought', *Journal of Asian and African Studies*, 45.

— (1999), 'Democratization in Sub-Saharan Africa: Faltering Prospects, New Hopes', *Journal of Contemporary African Studies*, 17(1).

Osundare, Niyi (1983), *Songs of the Marketplace*, Ibadan: New Horns Press.

Ousmane, Sembene (1970), *God's Bits of Wood* (trans. Frances Price), London: Heinemann.

— (1972), *The Money-order with White Genesis* (trans. Clive Wake), London: Heinemann.

— (1976), *Xala* (trans. Clive Wake), London: Heinemann.

Paige, Glenn D. (2000), 'Toward a Nonviolent 21st Century', *Journal of Future Studies*, 4(2), May.

Palmer, Eustace (1979), *The Growth of the African Novel*, London: Heinemann.

Parkinson, G. H. R. (1988), 'What is Philosophy?', in G. H. R. Parkinson (ed.), *An Encyclopaedia of Philosophy*, London: Routledge.

Petersen, Kirstein Holst and Anna Rutherford (eds) (1991), *Chinua Achebe: A Celebration*, Oxford and Portsmouth, NH: Heinemann.

Petrovsky, Vladimir (1990), 'New Thinking: Questions and Answers', *Political Science and Politics*, XXIII(1), March.

Pieterse, Cosmo and Donald Munro (eds) (1969), *Protest and Conflict in African Literature*, London: Heinemann.

Plant, Raymond (1998), 'Political Philosophy, Nature of', in Edward Craig (ed.), *Routledge Encyclopedia of Philosophy*, Vol. 7, London and New York: Routledge.

Plato (1941), *The Republic* (trans. with Introduction and Notes by Francis Macdonald Conford), London: Oxford University Press.

— (1973), 'The Death of Socrates', in G. Robert Carlsen and Gabriele L. Rico (eds), *Western Literature* (2nd edn), New York: Webster Division, McGraw-Hill.

Pocklington, Thomas C. (1970), 'Protest, Resistance, and Political Obligation', *Canadian Journal of Political Science*, III(1), March.

— (1975), 'Political Philosophy and Political Obligation', *Canadian Journal of Political Science*, VIII(4), December.

Poggioli, Renato (1963), 'Literature', *The American People's Encyclopedia*, Vol. 12, New York: Grolier Incorporated.

Popper, Karl (1963), *The Open Society and Its Enemies*, New York: Harper and Row.

Pratt, Cranford (1979), 'Tanzania's Transition to Socialism: Reflections of a Democratic Socialist', in B. U. Mwansasu and Cranford Pratt (eds), *Towards Socialism in Tanzania*, Toronto: University of Toronto Press.

Presbey, Gail M. (1996), 'Fanon on the Role of Violence in Liberation: A Comparison with Gandhi and Mandela', in Lewis R. Gordon et al. (eds), *Fanon: A Critical Reader*, Oxford: Blackwell Publishers.

— (2000), *The Philosophical Quest: A Cross-cultural Reader*, Boston, MA: McGraw Hill.

Przeworski, Adam (1992), 'The Neoliberal Fallacy', *Journal of Democracy*, 3(3), July.

Quayson, Ato (2000), *Post Colonialism: Theory, Practice or Process?* Cambridge: Polity Press and Blackwell Publishers.

Radcliff, Benjamin (2001), 'Politics, Markets, and Life Satisfaction: The Political Economy of Human Happiness', *American Political Science Review*, 95(4), December.

Randall, V. and Robin Theobold (1985), *Political Change and Under- Development*, Houndsmills: Macmillan Press.

Raphael, D. D. (1976), *Problems*

of Political Philosophy (rev. edn), London and Basingstoke: Macmillan.

Rathore, L. S. (1975), 'In Defence of Political Theory', Indian Journal of Political Science, XXXVI(4), October–December.

— (1976), 'The Nature of Political Theory', Indian Journal of Political Science, XXXVII(2), April–June.

Ripstein, Arthur (1997), 'Political Philosophy', in John V. Canfield (ed.), Routledge History of Philosophy: Philosophy of Meaning, Knowledge and Value in the Twentieth Century, Vol. X, London and New York: Routledge.

Rivers, Isabel (1991), 'Literature and the History of Ideas', in Martin Coyle et al. (eds), Encyclopedia of Literature and Criticism, London: Routledge.

Rosenstock-Huessy, Eugen (1963), 'William Ockham', The American People's Encyclopedia, Vol. 19, New York: Grolier Incorporated.

Rothchild, Donald (1969), 'Ethnic Inequalities in Kenya', Journal of Modern African Studies, 7(4).

Rowe, Christopher (1997), 'Plato: Aesthetics and Psychology', in C. C. Taylor (ed.), Routledge History of Philosophy: From the Beginning to Plato, Vol. 1, London and New York: Routledge.

Ruch, E. A. and K. C. Anyanwu (1981), African Philosophy: An Introduction to the Main Philosophical Trends in Contemporary Africa, Rome: Catholic Book Agency.

Ryan, Alan (1998), 'Political Philosophy', in A. C. Grayling (ed.), Philosophy 2: Further

Through the Subject, Oxford: Oxford University Press.

Sabine, George H. (1939), 'What is a Political Theory?', Journal of Politics, 1.

Salomon, Albert (1957), 'Sociology and the Literary Artist', in Stanley Romaine Hopper (ed.), Spiritual Problems in Contemporary Literature, New York: Harper and Brothers.

Sartre, Jean-Paul (1950), What is Literature? (trans. Bernard Frechtman), Guildford: Methuen and Co.

Schoolman, Morton (1973), 'Further Reflections on Work, Alienation, and Freedom in Marcuse and Marx', Canadian Journal of Political Science, VI(2), June.

Seaman, John W. (1978), 'L. T. Hobhouse and the Theory of "Social Liberalism"', Canadian Journal of Political Science XI(4), December.

Shearmur, Jeremy (1992), 'In Defense of Neo-liberalism', Journal of Democracy, 3(3), July.

Shively, Phillips W. (1997), Power and Choice: An Introduction to Political Science (5th edn), New York: McGraw-Hill.

Shivji, I. G. (1976), Class Struggles in Tanzania, London: Heinemann.

Sicherman, Carol (1995), 'Ngugi's Colonial Education: "The Subversion of the African Mind"', African Studies Review, 38(3), December.

Simpson, Chris (2002), 'Sowing the Seeds', BBC Focus on Africa, July–September.

Sklar, Richard L. (1965), 'Contradictions in the Nigerian Political System', Journal of Modern African Studies, 3(2).

— (ed.) (1994), Nationalism and

Development in Africa: Selected
Essays by James Smoot Coleman,
Berkeley: University of California
Press.

Skurnik, Walter A. E. (1965),
'Leopold Sédar Senghor and
African Socialism', Journal of
Modern African Studies, 3(3).

Small, Robin (1994), 'Nietzsche',
in C. L. Ten (ed.), Routledge
History of Philosophy: The
Nineteenth Century, Vol. VII,
London and New York:
Routledge.

So, Alvin Y. (1990), Social
Change and Development:
Modernization, Dependency and
World-system Theories, Newbury
Park, CA: Sage Publications.

Sogolo, Godwin (1981), 'Literary
Values and the Academic Mind:
A Portrait of the Humanistic
Studies', Ibadan Journal of
Humanistic Studies, 2, October.

Sole, Kelwyn (1988), 'The Days of
Power: Depictions of Politics and
Community in Four Recent South
African Novels', Research in
African Literatures, 19(1), Spring.

Southall, Roger (1999), 'Re-forming
the State? Kleptocracy and the
Political Transition in Kenya',
Review of African Political
Economy, 79(93–108), ROAPE
Publications.

Soyinka, Wole (1976), Myth,
Literature and the African
World, Cambridge: Cambridge
University Press.

— (1981), The Jero Plays: The
Trials of Brother Jero and
Jero's Metamorphosis, Ibadan:
Spectrum Books.

Spivak, Gayatri Chakravorty (1994),
'Can the Subaltern Speak?', in
P. Willams and L. Chrisman (eds),
Colonial Discourse and Post-

colonial Theory: A Reader, New
York: Columbia University Press.

Staniland, H. S. (1979), 'What is
Philosophy?', Second Order: An
African Journal of Philosophy,
VIII(1, 2), January–July.

Suberu, Rotimi T. (2001), 'Can
Nigeria's New Democracy
Survive?', Current History: A
Journal of Contemporary World
Affairs, 100(646), May.

Swainson, Nicola (1977) 'The Rise
of a National Bourgeoisie in
Kenya', RAPE, 8, January–April.

Swingewood, Alan (1975), The
Novel and Revolution, London
and Basingstoke: Macmillan.

Tamas, G. M. (1992), 'Socialism,
Capitalism and Modernity',
Journal of Democracy, 3(3), July.

Tassi, Aldo (1998), 'Philosophy
and Theatre,' International
Philosophical Quarterly,
XXXVIII(1), Issue 149, March.

Ten, C. L. (1988), 'The Limits of
the State', in G. R. H. Parkinson
(ed.), An Encyclopaedia of
Philosophy, London: Routledge.

Thigpen, Robert B. and Lyle A.
Downing (1982), 'A Critique of
Liberalism: The Application of
Unger's Knowledge and Politics
to Rawls's Theory of Justice',
Review of Politics, 44(1), January.

Thomas, Darryl (2001), 'Between
Globalization and Global
Apartheid: African Development
in the New Millennium',
International Journal of African
Studies, 3(1), Fall.

Thomson, Alex (2000), An Introduction to African Politics, London
and New York: Routledge.

Throup, D. W. (985), 'The Origins
of Mau Mau', African Affairs:
The Journal of the Royal African
Society, 84(336), July.

Tiffin, Helen (1995), 'Post-colonial Literatures and Counter-discourse', in Bill Ashcroft et al. (eds), *The Post-colonial Studies Reader*, London and New York: Routledge.

Tillman, Frank A., B. Berofsky and J. O'Connor (1971), *Introductory Philosophy*, New York: Harper and Row.

Townshend, Jules (1996), *The Politics of Marxism: The Critical Debates*, London and New York: Leicester University Press.

Turok, Ben (1987), *Africa: What Can be Done?*, London and New Jersey: Institute for African Alternatives and Zed Books.

Udenta, Udenta O. (1996), *Art, Ideology and Social Commitment in African Poetry: A Discourse*, Enugu, Nigeria: Fourth Dimension Publishers.

Ukoyen, Joseph (1993), 'Realism and the Novel: A Critical Reappraisal', *Ibadan Journal of Humanistic Studies*, 6, August.

Wagner, Harrison R. (1994), 'Peace, War, and the Balance of Power', *American Political Science Review*, 88(3), September.

Wallerstein, Immanuel (1979), *The Capitalist World-economy*, New York: Cambridge University Press.

Wallis, William (2002), 'Gridlock', *BBC Focus on Africa*, April–June.

Wautheir, Claude (1978), *The Literature and Thought of Modern Africa* (2nd English edn), London: Heinemann.

Weffort, Francisco C. (1992), 'The Future of Socialism', *Journal of Democracy*, 3(3), July.

White, Stephen (2003), 'Rethinking Postcommunist Transition', *Government and Opposition*, 38(4), Autumn.

Whittemore, Robert C. (1963), 'Philosophy', *The American People's Encyclopedia*, Vol. 15, New York: Grolier Incorporated.

Wilkinson, Jane (1992), *Talking with African Writers: Interviews with African Poets, Playwrights and Novelists*, Oxford and Portsmouth: James Currey and Heinemann.

Williams, Raymond (1977), *Marxism and Literature*, Oxford: Oxford University Press.

Wilson, Edmund (1972), 'Marxism and Literature', in David Lodge (ed.), *20th Century Literary Criticism: A Reader*, London: Longman.

Wren, Robert M. (1981), *Achebe's World: The Historical and Cultural Context of the Novels of Chinua Achebe*, Harlow: Longman.

Yai, Olabiyi (1977), 'Theory and Practice in African Philosophy: The Poverty of Speculative Philosophy', *Second Order: An African Journal of Philosophy*, VI(2), July.

Zwingina, Jonathan Silas (1972), *Capitalist Development in an African Economy*, Ibadan: Ibadan University Press.

Index

Index